BRITISH ARMY CAMPAIGN MEDALS

by

Robert W. D. Ball

Antique Trader Books
Dubuque, Iowa

ISBN: 0-930625-64-1

Library of Congress Catalog Card Number: 96-86493

Manufactured in the United States of America

Published by
Antique Trader Books
Dubuque, Iowa

Contents

Dedication

This book is dedicated to the officers and men of the British Imperial, Colonial, Indian, and Native Forces, both living and dead. These men unflinchingly marched, fought, bled and died for political reasons they scarcely understood. They did understand devotion to duty, honor and loyalty.

There are few spots on the face of the earth that have not felt the tread of British boots at one time or another, and it is this long history of war, conquest, and empire-building that is commemorated in the medals awarded the men who unfailingly followed their orders.

Acknowledgments

The empire is gone, but the heroic efforts of the British soldier live on, and the medals are there to silently speak for the dead.

When a book such as this is being organized, I never cease to be astounded and gratified by the open and willing assistance of old friends and acquaintances from the collecting world. Not only did they make their collections available to me, but their extensive knowledge. . . and constructive criticism. Without all of these, what you find between these covers would never have come to fruition.

Above all, without my old friend Joe Wupperfeld, the idea for this book would have died before it started. Joe's one great regret in life is that he wasn't born a Scotsman so he could have served at one time or another in every Scottish Regiment in the British Army! Among Joe's many collecting passions is his wonderful array of British Army medals, all of which are named to members of Scottish regiments. Joe is one of the truly generous men of the world, wanting to share his love of history and medals with fellow collectors, and for that, I thank him! Unless otherwise identified, all medals shown are from his collection.

Members of the Orders and Medals Society of America have provided rare medals for me to photograph, along with the information necessary to describe the award's background and the qualifications needed to merit it. My thanks to Jeff Floyd, Steve Johnson, Paul Peters, and others. Although we have never met, Mark Razanauskas willingly shipped me some of his treasured collection, purely on the advice of others. . . thanks for the trust, Mark! Loren Schave was happy to dismount many of his medals from the wall where they had hung for years. Without all of you, this book would have been so much more difficult to write. My thanks also to all the folks in the lab at Express Photo of Avon, Connecticut for all the care taken by them to ensure the quality of the photographs in this book.

Lastly, I must express my gratitude for the previous efforts of others interested in the field of medal collecting. The works produced by them over the years have been meticulously reviewed in my striving to make this book as accurate as possible.

You will notice that the medals in the contents of the book are in order according to the first year for which they would have been eligible to be awarded. The terms "clasp" and "bar" are used interchangeably within the body of the book and mean the same thing.

In many respects, this book has been not only a pleasure to write, but also rewarding on a personal level, for while I thought I knew a lot about British military history, my knowledge has been considerably enhanced and given far greater depth than I would have thought possible when I began my research years ago.

— **Robert W. D. Ball, 1996**

Foreword

From all that can be determined, the collecting of British medals in Great Britain was energized with the publishing of the three volume work by Carter, *Medals of the British Army*, in 1861. Interest was instant, and collecting surged. The 1890s ushered in the high point for medal collecting in Great Britain, with prominent collectors realizing the historical importance of preserving the earlier medals for posterity.

From the Anglo-Boer War, the Queen's South Africa Medal, with its many combinations of bars, caught the imagination of collectors around the world and also excited interest in the earlier medals. The First World War saw the first edition of Taprell Dorling's book *Ribbons and Medals*, which was so popular that it has gone into nine editions. Collecting soared during and after the war, and Dorling's book was a most valuable guide. As a boy in the 1930s, one of my first British medals came from the catalog of Francis Bannerman and Son, the Army-Navy dealers on lower Broadway in New York City. World War II further inspired the true collector, though, in all honesty, I do not feel the medals of World War II have the same intrinsic beauty as the earlier medals. In 1947, L. L. Gordon's *British Battles and Medals* first appeared, and by the fourth edition, proved to be one of the outstanding handbooks and guides to British military battles and the medals awarded as a result of those battles.

The collector of British Army medals finds much of the world's history cast into the medals he so proudly displays. In victory as well as in defeat, the British Army had a profound effect upon the course of history. In truth, at the height of the Empire, the sun really never did set upon British holdings around the world. In spite of the British attitude of "bearing the white man's burden," British administration of conquered territories and countries did instill a sense of democracy, as well as foster an improvement in government and public welfare. In truth, wherever the British boot trod, the country, in the long run, was the better for it.

Today, with territorial holdings greatly diminished, the history of British world exploits lives on in the beauty and significance of medals carefully cherished and preserved by the collector. My hope is that this work will be of value and assistance to the beginning as well as the more advanced collector, and that all will gain as much pleasure and added knowledge as I did in researching and writing this book.

The Military General Service Medal 1793-1814

With its complex history, this is one of the most interesting of all British campaign medals. The medal was issued for twenty-one years of service in war, but the authorized bars cover only thirteen years. The medal wasn't authorized until forty-six years after the first campaign it commemorates; it was issued fifty-five years after the first date on the medal; and then was presented only to survivors.

Lastly, this medal depicts the head of a sovereign not even born when many of the earlier engagements were fought. Ironically, it even became known as the "Dead Man's Medal." While veterans of Waterloo had their own medal to proudly display, other veterans of the Napoleanic Wars had nothing to show for their valiant service. It wasn't until British public opinion prevailed over the objections of the Duke of Wellington that the

Military General Service Medal, in silver, was finally instituted in 1847 and awarded in 1848, along with a total of twenty-eight clasps covering actions that took place between 1806 and 1814. In 1850, a further order provided a twenty-ninth clasp for "EGYPT, 1801." Some 26,000 of these medals were awarded, along with an almost infinite variety of 84,000 clasps. Medals with fifteen clasps each were received by two recipients, while more than 8,000 recipients were awarded only one clasp.

Due to the time lapse between the designated campaigns and the authorization date of the medal, a pitifully small number of survivors from each regiment were still alive to receive the award. In addition, many eligible survivors were not informed that the medal was available to them, or were unable to claim their award for other reasons. A majority of the clasps were for service during the Peninsula War of 1811-1814, with six clasps also being issued for the Peninsula War of 1808-1809. A total of three clasps were issued for service rendered in Canada; two clasps for service in the West Indies; and one each for Egypt (1801), Maida (southern Italy, 1806), and Java (1811).

Far Left—**Military General Service Medal, 1793-1814** (*Obverse*)

Left—**Military General Service Medal, w/bars "Toulsouse," "Orthes," "Pyrenees," "Salamanca," "Ciudad Rodrigo," "Fuentes D'onor," and "Busaco"** (*Reverse*)

The Battle of Busaco, showing French troops being driven from the ridge at bayonet point, 27 September 1810.
Drawing by Atkinson

The obverse of this medal, as designed by W. Wyon, depicts the head of Victoria Regina, facing to the left, with the word "VICTORIA" to the left of her head, and "REGINA" to the right. The date "1848" appears at the bottom of the bust. The reverse depicts a young Queen Victoria placing a laurel wreath on the head of the Duke of Wellington as he kneels before her holding his field marshal's baton. The British lion is depicted couchant at the side of Victoria's dais, with the words "TO THE" appearing to the left of Victoria, and "BRITISH ARMY" appearing at Wellington's right. In the exergue are the dates 1793-1814.

Surprisingly, some battles that one would assume to be included for clasps are omitted, such as the

The storming of Badajoz 6 April 1812. Author's collection

capture of the Cape of Good Hope from the Dutch in 1806; the brilliant victory at Kioge, outside of Copenhagen, in 1807; the passage of the Douro in the Peninsula; and the taking of St. Lucia in 1796.

Clasps were normally struck in groups of three where appropriate, and then riveted together. The medal is hung from a blue-edged crimson ribbon by means of a straight, swiveling suspension. It was often worn with the reverse displayed, and the obverse hidden from view. Naming of the medal is always in impressed Roman capitals around the rim. It is interesting, and important, to keep in mind that of those who fought in the various campaigns and battles and who were otherwise eligible for the award, only about ten percent actually received the medal! When the number of medals destroyed, lost, or housed in museum collections is taken into account, it's understandable why this medal is particularly desirable and scarce. ✕

British and French Officers exchanging drinks during a temporary armistice in the Peninsula War, 1809.
Author's collection

The twenty-nine authorized bars for the Military General Service Medal

"ALBUHERA"—6 May 1811

"BADAJOZ"—17 March - 6 April 1812

"BARROSA"—5 March 1811

"BENEVENTE"—29 December 1808

"BUSACO"—27 September 1810

"CHATEAUGUAY"—26 October 1813

"CHRYSTLER'S FARM"—11 November 1813

"CIUDAD RODRIGO"—8 - 9 January 1812

"CORUNNA"—16 January 1809

"EGYPT"—2 March to 2 September 1801

"FORT DETROIT"—August 1812

"FUENTES D'ONOR"—5 May 1811

"GUADALOUPE"—January and February 1810

"JAVA"—10 - 26 August 1811

"MAIDA"—4 July 1806

"MARTINIQUE"—30 January - 24 February 1809

"NIVE"—9 - 13 September 1813

"NIVELLE"—10 November 1813

"ORTHES"—27 February 1814

"PYRENEES"—25 July - 2 August 1813

"ROLEIA"—17 August 1808

"SAHAGUN"—21 December 1808

"SAHAGUN & BENEVENTE"—Awarded to those present at both actions

"ST. SEBASTIAN"—17 July - 8 September 1813

"SALAMANCA"—22 July 1812

"TALAVERA"—27 and 28 July 1809

"TOULOUSE"—10 April 1814

"VIMIERA"—21 August 1808

"VITTORIA"—21 June 1813

The Army Of India Medal 2 1799–1826

This medal, which collectors call the First India Medal, was authorized 28 February 1851, and was issued only to survivors of the campaigns and battles that took place throughout India between 1803 and 1826. The medal was the counterpart of the Military General Service Medal for Imperial troops on active service in India. Campaign service, disease, and old age left few men able to actually collect the award. Twenty-one clasps were eventually authorized, and the medal was never issued without a clasp, or without a name. Contrary to the customary practice, clasps for this medal are read from the top down, with the most recent clasp at the bottom, closest to the medal. There are many clasp combinations, with any medal bearing more than one clasp considered a rarity.

The author has been unable to determine the exact number of medals awarded. As an example, over 40,000 men fought in the six general actions that constituted the First Mahratta War, for which clasps were awarded, but less than two hundred men were left alive to claim their medals. Before the battle of Deig, the 1st Bengal European Regiment (later named the Royal Munster Fusiliers) had over eight hundred men on the rolls just prior to the battle, while only three men were alive to claim their medals in 1851.

On the obverse of this medal is the head of Queen Victoria, facing left, with the legend "VICTORIA REGINA." The reverse features a seated, winged figure of Victory holding a laurel wreath in one hand and a wreath in the other. A palm tree is in the background. Above are the words "TO THE ARMY OF

Army Of India Medal, 1799-1826, bar "Maheidpoor" (Obverse)

Army Of India Medal (Reverse)

INDIA," while the dates "1799-1826" are in the exergue at the bottom. The medal is suspended from a light blue ribbon that passes through an ornamental scroll suspension at the top of the medal.

The twenty-one clasps for the Army of India Medal are as follows, with the number awarded to Europeans shown in brackets following the name of the battle:

"ALLIGHUR" [66]—4 September 1803. First Mahratta War, the storming of Fort Allighur.

"BATTLE OF DELHI" [40]—11 September 1803. The defeat by Lord Lake of the 20,000-man Scinde Army.

"ASSAYE" [87]—23 September 1803. The defeat by Wellington's 4,000-man army of the French-led native army of 50,000.

"ASSEERGHUR" [48]—21 October 1803. The surrender of Fort Asseerghur.

"LASWARREE" [100]—1 November 1803. The defeat, with very heavy casualties, of the Mahratta Army that was marching to recapture Delhi.

"ARGAUM" [126]—29 November 1803. Battle on the plains of Argaum.

"GAWILGHUR"[110]—15 December 1803. The siege and surrender of the fortress of Gawilghur.

The Battle of Assaye, 23 September 1803. Wm. Heath

"DEFENCE OF DELHI" [5]—8-14 October 1804. The defence of Delhi against the attempts by Holkar to recapture the city.

"BATTLE OF DEIG" [47]—13 November 1804. A hotly-fought battle near the River Jumna.

"CAPTURE OF DEIG" [0]—11-23 December 1804. Siege and storming of the fortress of Deig.

"NEPAUL" [505]—October 1814-March 1816. Awarded for the two-year campaign against the Gurkhas.

"KIRKEE" [5]—5 November 1817. The defeat of the 26,000-man Mahratta army near Poona.

"POONA" [75]—11-16 November 1817. The capture of Poona.

"KIRKEE AND POONA" [88]—Awarded to troops who were engaged in both actions.

"SEETABULDEE" [1]— 26-27 November 1817. Although this clasp was authorized, there is some doubt whether or not the clasp was claimed. Awarded for the defeat of the army of the Rajah of Berar near the city of Nagpore.

"NAGPORE" [155]—16 December 1817. Siege and capture of the city of Nagpore.

"SEETABULDEE AND NAG-PORE" [21]—Awarded to troops involved in both actions.

"MAHEIDPOOR" [75]—21 December 1817. For the battle against the Pindarries.

"CORYGAUM" [4]—1 January 1818. The successful defence of a British column against the almost overwhelming attack by 28,000 enemy cavalry and infantry.

"AVA" [2,325]—1824-1826. Awarded to those troops involved in the campaign in Burma. This was the only clasp for which the Royal Navy qualified.

"BHURTPOOR" [1,059]—17-18 January 1826. Awarded to those troops involved in the successful storming of the city of Bhurtpoor. There were no clasps authorized for earlier (in 1803) attempts to take the same city. Believed by most to be impregnable, Bhurtpoor was garrisoned by 20,000 enemy troops, and a wall seven miles in circumference. A 10,000-pound mine made of black powder was set off under the city walls, and storming columns rushed into the breech, with the "forlorn hope" carrying a black flag signifying that no quarter was to be given. This was typical of the fighting of this period, commemorated by the clasps to this medal. ✕

Top—**Army Of India Medal, 1799-1826, bar "Ava"** *(Reverse)*

Bottom—**Army Of India Medal** *(Obverse)*

Mark Razanauskas Collection

Waterloo Medal 18 June 1815

The course of history was changed by the battle of Waterloo, but Waterloo was also responsible for a medal for all ranks who served at the battles of Ligny, Quatre Bras and Waterloo, 16-18 June 1815. This medal is notable for three reasons: It was the first medal awarded to all soldiers regardless of rank; the first campaign medal given to the soldier's next-of-kin for those killed in action; and the first medal to have the name of the recipient impressed around the rim by machine.

Approximately 39,000 medals were awarded; however, few of these are uncovered today. Six thousand medals were issued to Cavalry; 4,000 to Guards; 16,000 to Line Regiments; 5,000 to the Artillery. In addition, 6,500 were awarded to the men of the King's German Legion, who played an important part in the battle, and who suffered heavy casualties. There were also supply personnel who were issued the medal.

The obverse of the medal (which was always in silver) depicts the head of the Prince Regent, facing left, wearing a laurel wreath, and the inscribed legend "GEORGE P./REGENT." The reverse depicts the Grecian winged figure of Victory, seated, holding a palm branch in her right hand and an olive branch in her left. Above the head of Victory is the word "WELLINGTON," while at the feet of Victory, in a rectangle, appears the word "WATERLOO." Below the rectangle is the date "June 18, 1815" in two lines. The figure of Victory, first appearing on the Waterloo medal, was incorporated into many future British medals.

Waterloo Medal (Obverse)

Waterloo Medal (Reverse)

The ribbon for the medal is crimson, with .25" wide, dark blue edges. Naming of the medal is always impressed in the rim in Roman capital letters, and always includes the regiment or the unit; the blank spaces are usually filled by two or three stars. The medal is suspended from the ribbon by means of a steel ring that is passed through a clip sweated to the top of the medal. These medals were worn proudly by the Waterloo veterans, even on their civilian clothing. Because many of the steel rings eventually rusted through, they were often replaced by rings of the veteran's own design, causing a collector to wonder exactly what he has discovered. ✕

Wellington orders the general advance at Waterloo. R. Boyer

Waterloo, late afternoon. Wm. Heath

Meeting of Wellington and Blucher at La Belle Alliance.
George Jones

South Africa Campaign Medal 1834–1853

Granted by General Order 22 November 1854, this medal commemorates the success of Her Majesty's Forces in campaigns dealing with the suppression of the Kaffirs in eastern South Africa during the periods 1834-35, 1846-47 and between 24 December 1850 and 6 February 1853. This medal, of which there were approximately 9,500 awarded, was issued without a clasp and with the date "1853" in the reverse exergue. The only way to determine the specific campaign for which a medal was awarded is to research the recipient in the regimental rolls; however, since some of these medals were issued to men of the Naval Brigade, and only showed name and rank, this is not always possible. While confusing to collectors, it was probably equally so to the recipient!

The first campaign in 1834 was against the nomadic and plundering Kaffirs at the extreme eastern end of the Cape Colony. It was decided to punish the most troublesome of the tribes. A column commanded by Major-General Benjamin D'Urban, K.C.B., was formed, with Sir Harry G. Smith as Second-in-Command (Smith later became Governor of the Colony; his wife gave her name to the town "Ladysmith," which gained fame in the second Boer War). Suppression required great endurance and tact on the part of the British as they did not wish to incite other tribes to violence. Peace was achieved through a treaty signed in April 1835.

In April 1846, another expedition was required to put down the depredations of the Gaika Kaffirs being led by Chief Sandilli. By this time, the Gaika Kaffirs had been equipped with arms and ammunition by traders, so the two small British forces involved suffered a number of casualties before the surrender of Sandilli and his tribe in October 1846.

In December of 1850, Chief Sandilli was again up to his old tricks, causing much trouble for the British. To their consternation Sir Harry Smith was even penned up in Fort Cox, with ensuing inconvenience and casualties for

South Africa Campaign Medal, 1834-1853 *(Obverse)*

South Africa Campaign Medal *(Reverse)*

the British forces. Sir Harry was replaced by Sir George Cathcart, and the campaign rolled on—the tribes eventually being driven into the mountains where they were split into small bands and finally forced to surrender on 20 December 1852, with peace being declared on 12 March 1853.

While in the process of reinforcing the units in South Africa during the final of the campaigns, the British troopship Birkenhead struck a rock and sank. During the disaster, all British officers and men aboard ship were drawn up in formation so the women and children could be evacuated to lifeboats, and it was in formation that many went down with the ship! This deed so inspired King Wilhelm of Prussia that he had the full story read to every unit of the Prussian army while on parade!

On the obverse of the medal is the diademed head of young Queen Victoria, looking left, with the legend "VICTORIA REGINA." The reverse shows a lion crouching near a mimosa bush, with "SOUTH AFRICA" above and the date "1853" in the exergue. The 1.25" wide ribbon is watered orange with two broad and two narrow stripes of dark blue. Suspension is by an ornamental swiveling suspender and claw clip sweated to the medal. The recipient's name and regiment are impressed on the edge of the medal in Roman capitals.

The medal was only given to survivors of the forces engaged in these campaigns. ✕

Ghuznee Medal
21-23 July 1839

The storming of the Afghan fortress of Ghuznee appears to have set a pattern for the prolific honors and awards that came with the First Afghan War. The commander-in-chief received a peerage, field officers and above were awarded the Order of the Dooranee Empire, and all ranks received the Ghuznee Medal. In addition, each of the eleven regiments involved in the action was given a battle honor. This was only the second medal awarded to British troops—the first having been the Waterloo Medal.

The Shah Soojah-ool-Mook, who was widely seen as staunchly pro-British, had been dethroned and exiled by the Persians. Seeing this as an excellent opportunity to extend the British sphere of influence, a column of British troops was despatched forthwith to right this obvious wrong. During their advance on Kabul, the Bombay Column stormed the fortress of Ghuznee with only minor (less than 150) casualties, which quickly and effectively ended resistance to the British and restored the Shah Soojah to the throne.

In grateful appreciation, the Shah ordered this medal struck and presented to all those present at the storming of the fortress. Unfortunately, he died before this could be accomplished, and the government of India eventually had to bear the entire cost. The medal was struck in silver only. Many variations will be found in the naming of the medal, since this was done at the recipient's expense, either on the rim or on the space left blank.

The obverse of the medal has a depiction of the fortress of

Ghuznee Medal (Obverse)

Ghuznee Medal (Reverse)

Ghuznee, with the name below in a curved exergue, while the reverse bears a mural crown below the mid-point, with the date "23rd JULY" at the top and the year "1839" at the bottom—the whole is surrounded by a laurel wreath with a space for the recipient's name. The medal is 1.46" in diameter. The ribbon, originally vertically half-green and half-yellow, was changed to the present color of half-crimson and half-

green. A straight suspender and attachment were sweated to the top of the medal.

Apparently there were two separate dies used to strike the medal, since one version has a much wider border than the other, while another style has a narrower and taller fortress. Five British regiments were present at the storming of Ghuznee, along with Europeans serving with the East India Company. ✕

First China War Medal
5 July 1840 – 29 August 1842

Almost impossible to believe today, the First China War, more popularly known as "The Opium War," was not fought to keep the "heathen" Chinese from slowly killing themselves and ruining their country with drugs, but, on the contrary, was fought to make sure that British merchants maintained a monopoly on the importation of drugs from India! The Chinese government banned the import of drugs of any type; destroyed the British warehouses that contained huge stocks of opium; and refused to pay any compensation.

The British Commissioner and residents were forced to flee Canton on 24 May 1839. Hong Kong was taken by the British on 23 August 1839, and later ceded to Britain on 20 January 1841. The blockade of Canton began on 28 June 1840, and it was carried out by a small British force from Madras, India, consisting of the 18th, 26th, 49th, 55th, and 98th Foot, along with Bengal Artillery and Sappers, and elements of the Bengal Volunteers.

The entire coastline of China was blockaded, and at one point the Chinese government offered a bounty of 40,000 dollars for an Englishman—dead or alive! A bewildering number of attacks and engagements took place before an ironic treaty of "Perpetual Friendship" was signed on 29 August 1842. Along with the island of Hong Kong, the British also received five trading bases, the most important of which were Canton and Shanghai.

The obverse of the medal carries the diademed head of Queen Victoria, with the legend "VICTORIA REGINA." The initial reverse of the medal—showing a British lion savaging a Chinese dragon—was considered to be too insensitive to the Chinese. The reverse design ultimately depicted a trophy of arms with an oval shield centered with the Royal Arms, positioned under a palm tree. Above is the inscription "ARMIS EXPOSCERE PACEM." In the exergue is the word "CHINA" and the date "1842" underneath. The 1.50" wide ribbon has yellow edges, with a .90" wide crimson stripe down the middle. Suspension is effected by a German silver straight suspender, sweated directly to the medal. The medal is named in bold capitals, with blank spaces filled with stars. There were no bars issued for this medal. ✕

First China War Medal, 1840-1842 (Obverse)

First China War Medal (Reverse)

Jellalabad Medal
First Afghan War
12 November 1841 – 7 April 1842

With the murder of the British envoy in Kabul, the First Afghan War commenced, and several British outposts, including Jellalabad, were attacked and brought under siege. At Jellalabad, the defenders had to contend not only with the wily Afghans, but also with short rations, treason, and earthquake shocks that destroyed one-third of the town itself and some of the defences. The garrison, numbering about 2,600 men, was made up of the 13th Foot, one regiment of Bengal Native Infantry, several other native detachments, and some loyal Afghan troops.

The Jellalabad Medal was produced in two issues. The first, minted in Calcutta and known as the "Mural Crown" issue, was thought to have been too crudely manufactured. Therefore, it was decided to mint the second issue known as the "Flying Victory," in London. Recipients of the first medal were offered an exchange; however there were few takers, the result being that the second issue is more rare than the first.

The first "Mural Crown" issue has a crown and the inscription "JELLALABAD" on the obverse, while the reverse has the date "VII/APRIL/1842" in three lines. This was the date that the siege was abandoned after the besieged made a determined attack on their besiegers. The medal can be suspended by either a straight steel suspender fitted directly to the rim of the medal, or held by a ring fitted to the medal rim. The style of naming varies considerably, and the name may appear on the obverse face under the mural crown, or along the edge of the medal. Apparently, the medal was

Jellalabad Medal, 1842 *(Obverse)*

Jellalabad Medal *(Reverse)*

also issued unnamed. The ribbon, which is common to both issues, is a rainbow-pattern watered red, white, yellow, white, and blue.

The second issue—the "Flying Victory"—was issued in March 1845, mainly because there had not been a sufficient number of the first issue produced, and the Governor General of India was very dissatisfied with the crude appearance of the first issue. The second medal, which was designed by W. Wyon, was struck at the Royal Mint in London. On the obverse is the diademed head of

young Queen Victoria with the legend "VICTORIA VINDEX"— very few medals were struck with the legend "VICTORIA REGINA." The reverse has a winged figure of Victory with a laurel wreath in her right hand and the staff of a Union Jack in the left hand, while flying over the fortress of Jellalabad. On the curve of the upper half of the medal is the inscription "JELLAL-ABAD VII APRIL." Below, in the exergue appears the date "MDCC-CXLII." The name of the recipient is indented in block letters on the rim of the medal. ✕

Defence Of Kelat-I-Ghilzie
February – May 1842

Minted only in silver, this medal was instituted by General Order, October 1842. It was awarded to the approximately 900 defenders of the fort Kelat-I-Ghilzie, located between Kabul and Kandahar. Only fifty or so members of this garrison were Europeans—the balance of the force being comprised mostly of Indian troops. Their force consisted of seven staff officers, eighty-six men of the 4/2 Bengal Artillery, twenty-three men from the 2nd and 3rd Bengal Sappers and Miners, two hundred and fifty men of the 43rd Bengal Native Infantry, and five hundred seventy men of the 3rd Shah Soojah's Infantry. The latter performed so valiantly that the regiment was absorbed into the Bengal Army in its entirety! Relief of the fort was accomplished on 26 May 1842 by the forces of General Nott. When issued to a named recipient, this is a very rare medal.

It appears that the designers of this medal tried to cram everything Victorian into their design! On the obverse, a laurel wreath encloses an ornamental shield, upon which is inscribed "KELAT-I-GHILZIE" in three lines, with the whole surmounted by a mural crown. On the reverse there is a trophy of arms, which includes a cuirass surmounted by a carabi-

Defence Of Kelat-I-Ghilzie Medal, 1842 (Obverse)

Defence Of Kelat-I-Ghilzie Medal (Reverse) Steve Johnson Collection

neer's helmet, placed above a plaque occupying the lower half of the reverse. The plaque bears the Latin inscription "INVICTA MDCCCXLII." Suspension is by means of a straight suspender pinned to an ungainly clip sweat-

ed to the top of the medal. The 1.75" wide ribbon is red, white, yellow, white, and blue in watered rainbow pattern, and it passes through the suspender. The recipient's name is engraved in script on the medal's edge. ✕

Candahar, Cabul and Ghuznee Medals
First Afghan War
October 1842 – October 1843

In commemoration of the confused fighting that occurred on the border of North West India and Afghanistan, the Candahar, Ghuznee and Cabul Medals were sanctioned by a General Order in October 1842. There were four different strikings (and two rarities), but only one medal could be awarded to any one man. The obverse of each medal is the same; however, the reverse shows the battle or battles in which the participant served.

The obverse face of the medal bears the familiar head of young Queen Victoria wearing a diadem, with the inscription "VICTORIA VINDEX." The reverse of each medal is as follows:

1. "CANDAHAR," with the date "1842" underneath, surrounded by a laurel wreath which is surmounted with a crown.

2. "CABUL," again with the date "1842" underneath, surrounded by a laurel wreath surmounted by a crown.

3. A pair of intertwined laurel wreaths almost forming two circles, with "GHUZNEE" in the first circle and "CABUL" in the second. The date "1842" appears below, while the whole is surmounted by a crown.

4. Includes the words "CANDAHAR, GHUZNEE, CABUL," and the date "1842" on four separate lines, surrounded by a laurel wreath and surmounted by a crown.

The two rare examples referred to earlier have a legend on the obverse which reads "VICTORIA REGINA" and also have the word "CABUL" spelled as "CABVL."

The 1.75" wide ribbon is a rainbow-pattern watered red, white, yellow, white, and blue. The medal is suspended by means of a straight steel suspender attached to the medal by a steel clip. These medals will generally be found named in script, while some will be in indented capitals. Others have been discovered that were never named. ✕

"The Remnants of an Army." Dr. Brydon reaches Jellalabad, 1842. Painting by Lady Butler

Top—**Candahar Medal, First Afghan War** *(Obverse)*

Bottom—**Candahar Medal, First Afghan War** *(Reverse)*

Steve Johnson Collection

Top—**Cabul Medal, First Afghan War** *(Obverse)*

Bottom—**Cabul Medal, First Afghan War** *(Reverse)*

Steve Johnson Collection

Top—**Ghuznee And Cabul Medal, First Afghan War** *(Obverse)*

Bottom—**Ghuznee And Cabul Medal, First Afghan War** *(Reverse)*

Mark Razanauskas Collection

Scinde Campaign Medals
6 January – 24 March 1843

Following close on the heels of the earlier Afghan War, this expedition by Major General Sir Charles Napier was intended to punish the Amirs of Scinde, Rustram, Nasir Khan and Shere Mahomed for their continual raiding of British convoys en route to and from Afghanistan. With a force numbering only 2,800 men and twelve guns, on 17 February 1843 Sir Charles, at the battle of Meeanee, defeated 30,000 troops of the Scinde infantry that were supported by 5,000 cavalry and fifteen guns.

One month later, after an epic march of eighty days across the desert and pulling the guns by hand, Sir Charles defeated a force of 20,000 troops of Meer Shere Mahomed at Dubba, located on the outskirts of Hyderabad. The only British regiment at both battles was the 22nd Foot (Cheshires), which suffered more than two hundred killed or wounded.

As happened in some battles in the preceding Indian Campaigns, there were three different strikings of the same medal, with only the reverses of the silver medals showing a difference.

In all examples, the obverse of the medal is the same. It carries the diademed head of a young Queen Victoria and the legend "VICTORIA REGINA." On the reverse of the first strike is the single word "MEEANEE" above the date "1843," surmounted by a crown and surrounded by a laurel wreath. This medal is extremely rare, as very few were issued to Europeans—the 22nd Foot receiving a total of sixty-five.

Scinde Campaign Medal *(Obverse)*

Scinde Campaign Medal *(Reverse)*

The second strike bears the word "HYDERABAD" above the date "1843" surmounted by a crown and surrounded by a laurel wreath. This, too, must be considered a rare medal.

The third strike bears the words "MEEANNE, HYDERABAD" and "1843" on three lines, surmounted by a crown and surrounded by a laurel wreath. This is also rare. The ribbon is 1.75" wide, rainbow-patterned watered red, white, yellow, white, and blue—the Military Ribbon of India. Suspension is by means of a ring or a straight steel suspender pinned through a steel clip sweated to the medal. The Commanding Officer of the 22nd Foot, at his own expense, paid for the replacement of the steel suspenders with silver ones. Naming of the medals is in block letters, although some are to be found lettered in script. There were no bars issued with this medal. ✕

Gwalior Campaign Stars
December 1843

Because of great reluctance shown by the Regent of the Mahratta State of Gwalior, Dada Khasgee Walla, to refrain from hurling insults at the British, a campaign was instituted under the leadership of Sir Hugh Gough to punish the impudent upstarts. This campaign was one the shortest on record in India, with both battles in the campaign having been waged on the same day.

Two columns of British and native soldiers entered the State of Gwalior, and two battles were fought on 29 December 1843, with the major battle centered around the village of Maharajpoor, which was strongly entrenched with 18,000 Mahrattas equipped with fifty guns. While slightly inferior in troop strength and number of guns, the British force under Sir Hugh Gough, after severe hand-to-hand fighting, was able to drive the foe from their defensive positions. The Mahratta artillerymen displayed both courage and gallantry—many of them having been bayoneted at their guns.

On the same afternoon, a second column, actually the left wing of the army under the command of General Grey, found the Mahrattas entrenched in the hills outside of the town of Punniar. Another bloody battle took place that finally broke the back of Mahratta resistance to the British. It was a costly price to pay for having insulted the British Raj!

The medal is a bronze six-pointed star, 1.70" wide and 2" high, made, appropriately, from melted-down cannon captured from the Mahrattas. The centerpiece is a small silver star of the same pattern, in the center of which is the date "29th DECr." in two lines, and in a circle around the date is the name of the particular battle, either "PUNNIAR" or "MAHARAJPOOR" and the year "1843." The reverse of this medal is plain, and it is on this face that the name is impressed, almost always in script. ✕

Top—**Gwalior Star, Maharajpoor** *(Obverse)*

Bottom—**Gwalior Star, Maharajpoor** *(Reverse)*

Mark Razanauskas Collection

Top—**Gwalior Star, Punniar** *(Obverse)*

Bottom—**Gwalior Star, Punniar** *(Reverse)*

Steve Johnson Collection

Sutlej Campaign Medal
The Sikh Wars
18 December 1845 – 22 February 1846

One of the most powerful and well-armed military forces on the Indian continent was the Sikh army, trained and led in many cases by European officers. This army was also extremely well equipped with the latest artillery. On 11 December 1845, the Sikh army—100,000 strong—unexpectedly crossed the Sutlej and invaded the Punjab with the intent of capturing both Ferozepore and Ludihana. Taken completely by surprise, Sir Hugh Gough, the Commander-in-Chief, was forced to march his men some one hundred fifty miles from Imballa. The invading army, which outnumbered the British forces by five-to-one, was met at Moodkee. After heavy fighting, resulting in many casualties for both sides, the Sikhs withdrew, leaving seventeen guns in the hands of the British.

Just three days later, on 21 December 1845, and now reinforced by the addition of two battalions of British troops, General Gough engaged the main Sikh army at Ferozeshuhur. This action, accompanied by ferocious losses on both sides, lasted for two days, with the British ultimately victorious on the battlefield, but having lost one out of every six men. One month later, another Sikh army crossed over the border and was stopped and defeated at the village of Aliwal. Sir Harry Smith was in command of the British force that took just three hours to rout the Sikhs from the field of battle, leaving all their guns behind in the course of their withdrawal. It was during this battle that the 16th Lancers won battle honors for gallantly charging and breaking an enemy square.

7th Bengal Light Cavalry, 1845. *Print by Henry Martens*

The end of this short campaign was realized when British forces met the 34,000-man-strong Sikh army entrenched at Sobraon, with an additional 20,000 men in reserve, all being supported by an artillery complement of seventy guns. Once more the Sikh army was defeated in battle, fleeing in total rout over the only bridge that spanned the Sutlej River at this point. The parapets of the bridge collapsed, and thousands of Sikh warriors were drowned,

Sutleg Campaign Medal
(Obverse)

**Sutleg Campaign Medal, Moodke,
1845** *(Reverse)*
Mark Razanauskas Collection

Sutleg Campaign Medal, Aliwal, 1846
(Reverse)

**The Battle of
Ferozeshuhur.**
Wupperfeld collection

bringing the Sutlej campaign to an end. The only regiments present as a whole for the four battles were the 31st and 50th Foot, the 24th and 47th Bengal Native Infantry, and the 5th Bengal Light Cavalry.

This medal was the first campaign medal sanctioned for both officers and enlisted men alike, with clasps. This medal also set a standard for design that has been generally followed ever since. The obverse bears the diademed head of young Queen Victoria with the legend "VICTORIA REGINA." The reverse bears the standing figure of Victory, facing left, and holding a wreath in her outstretched right hand. In her left hand rests an olive branch.

The 31st Regt. at the Battle of Sobraon, 10 February 1846.

Officer of the Bundelkhand Legion, 1847.
Print by Henry Marten

16th Lancers at Aliwal, 28 January 1846.
Print by Henry Martens

At her feet is a collection of trophies. The legend "ARMY OF THE SUTLEJ" appears around the circumference of the medal. Four different inscriptions are seen in the exergue, as follows:

(1) "MOODKEE 1845"

(2) "FEROZESHUHUR 1845"

(3) "ALIWAL 1846"

(4) "SOBRAON 1846"

The first action in which the recipient took part is named in the exergue. Three bars were issued, each bearing the name of the last three battles. Therefore, a man who had been in action for every action received a medal for "MOODKEE 1845" plus three bars, while a recipient who had fought only in the last battle received the medal with the exergue "SOBRAON 1846" without any bars. The medal hangs from a beautifully designed ornamental swiveling suspender, sweated to the medal. The 1.25" wide ribbon is dark blue and has crimson edges. The naming is in indented capital letters, or in light Roman skeleton lettering. ✕

Officers of the Bengal Horse Artillery, 1846.
Print by Henry Martens

Punjab Campaign Medal
7 September 1848 – 14 March 1849

The Punjab campaign became the third and final campaign in the subjugation of the Sikhs; in fact, it was a continuation of the Sutlej War which had left the militant Sikhs in a state of constant unrest and turmoil, and harboring unmitigated hatred for the British. The Sikhs continued to pose a threat to British interests in northern India despite defeats inflicted by British forces in 1845-46, leading to a third and final campaign being conducted against them after the murder of the British Resident at Mooltan, in 1848.

Two armies were fielded by the British, with one column of 28,000 men under the command of Major General Whish besieging the fortress of Mooltan, while Lord Gough led the second column northward to the Punjab. At Chilianwallah, a Sikh army under Sher Singh held well-fortified positions. On 13 January, Lord Gough reached these entrenchments and a major battle ensued, with the British losing several colors, four guns, and about 15% of their total strength. Both sides were savaged during the battle and they withdrew, exhausted, to their respective camps during three days of torrential rainstorms. Sher Singh's army, severely mauled, struck camp and made off for Lahore. Meanwhile, Mooltan had been stormed and the force under command of General Whish's moved to link up with Lord Gough's troops. The combined British force of 24,000 men and ninety-six guns caught up with the Sikh army at Goojerat on 20 February, completely routing them after a morning battle. The Sikhs surrendered, and the Punjab was annexed.

All forces to see service in the Punjab were granted a medal by General Order dated 2 April 1849. The obverse of the medal bears the diademed head of young Queen Victoria, inscribed with the legend "VICTORIA REGINA." The reverse of the medal is highly detailed, depicting the Sikh army surrendering their arms and colors to Major General Sir Walter Gilbert, who is shown on horseback. Against the backdrop of a hill with palm trees, two regiments of East India Company troops are drawn-up in review in the middle background. Around the top is the inscription "TO THE

Punjab Campaign Medal (Obverse)

Punjab Campaign Medal (Reverse)

ARMY OF THE PUNJAB," while in the exergue is the date "MDCC-CXLIX." The ribbon is dark blue with a yellow stripe on each side, and is suspended from an ornate swiveling suspender sweated to the medal. Names are impressed in Roman capitals; however, those issued to native troops were usually done in an uneven manner, or in running script.

Clasps were issued for the three principal actions: "MOOLTAN," for those involved in the siege from 7 September 1848 to 22 January 1849 (2,900 clasps issued to Europeans); and clasps for the two main battles, "CHILIAN-WALA" (4,300 clasps awarded to Europeans) and "GOOJERAT," (6,200 clasps to Europeans). Many of these medals were issued without clasps, and the maximum number of clasps one man could be awarded was two. Clasps were to be read downwards; that is, the last award was closest to the medal.

At the Battle of Chilianwala, the 24th Foot lost twenty-one officers and five hundred and three other ranks—losses greatly out of proportion to those suffered by other regiments—and these medals are therefore highly prized by collectors. An interesting side note to this campaign is the fact that the Sikhs later became the most loyal troops in the army of "John Company"—standing shoulder-to-shoulder with British comrades throughout the Indian Mutiny, and constituting the most reliable regiments throughout their long history with the British army. ⨯

Indian General Service Medal 1854-1895

On 22 December 1853, this medal, with "PEGU" clasp, was authorized for Her Majesty's—as well as the East Indies Company's—land and sea forces engaged in the Burma War of 1852-53. Subsequent to its authorization, this medal was also issued in commemoration of a number of engagements that took place on the Indian frontier, as well as the expedition to the Malay Peninsula. Each campaign is indicated by a separate clasp. With the addition of a second clasp, the newest clasp is placed closest to the medal, with the sole exception of the clasp for "PEGU," which always remains next to the medal.

The obverse of the medal bears the diademed head of Queen Victoria, with the legend "VICTORIA REGINA." The reverse bears the standing figure of Victory, shown crowning a classical warrior with a laurel wreath. The warrior is seated, with a short sword in his right hand and a scabbard in his left. A Roman helmet is on the ground at his side, along with a shield. In the exergue is a lotus flower and leaves. The medal is suspended from a 1.25" red ribbon with two dark blue stripes. The suspender is a silver scroll bar and claw clip similar to that used for the Sutlej and Punjab medals. The junction of the suspender, claw clip, and all the bars are covered by a lotus flower rosette.

Indian General Service Medal, 1854-1895, bar "Hazara" (Obverse)

Indian General Service Medal, 1854-1895 (Reverse)

Men of the 2nd Bn., Seaforth Highlanders, during the Black Mountain expedition.

Wupperfeld collection

Twenty-three different clasps were issued with the India 1854 medal, as follows:

"PEGU"—28 March 1852-30 June 1853. The Second Burma campaign.

"PERSIA"—5 December 1856-8 February 1857. War with Persia was declared, with a combined Army and Naval force entering Eastern Persia.

"NORTH WEST FRONTIER"—3 December 1849-22 October 1868. Awarded to all survivors of the fifteen different campaigns that took place over nineteen years. This included those involved in the advance in the Hazara Campaign of 1868.

"UMBELYA"—20 October-23 December 1863. Issued for an expeditionary force sent into Hindustan.

"BHOOTAN"—December 1864-February 1863. Awarded to a punitive force of four columns that entered the state of Bhootan to avenge an insult to the head of a British mission.

"LOOSHAI"—9 December 1871-20 February 1872. Granted to native troops composing the Looshai Expeditionary Force employed against the Looshai tribes. No British troops were involved.

"PERAK"—2 November 1875-20 March 1876. This clasp was granted to the forces engaged against the Malays; a British naval brigade was involved.

"JOWAKI 1877-8"—9 November 1877-19 January 1878. Clasp awarded to those troops engaged in putting down the Afridi tribesmen who were objecting to a new road running through their territory.

"NAGA 1879-80"—December 1879-January 1880. This clasp was awarded for operations against the tribes in the Naga Hills.

"BURMA 1885-7"—14 November 1885-30 April 1887. This clasp was awarded to those involved in operations during the annexation of Burma.

"SIKKIM 1888"—15 March-27 September 1888. Clasp awarded to survivors of the expedition to Sikkim, adjacent to Tibet, where Tibetans had been building forts.

"HAZARA 1888"—3 October-9 November 1888. Awarded to those members of the Hazara Field Force in the expedition against the Black Mountain tribes.

"BURMA 1887-89"—1 May 1887-31 March 1889. Authorized for survivors of expeditions that had been conducted to suppress large-scale banditry.

"CHIN LUSHAI 1889-90"—15 November 1889-30 April 1890. Awarded to all the survivors of two columns: the Burma column operating against the Chins and the Chittagong column against the Lushai.

"SAMANA 1891"—5 April-25 May 1891. This bar was awarded to members of the Miranzi Expeditionary Force. This column operated against fanatics in the Miranzi Valley and the Samana Heights.

"HAZARA 1891"—12 March-16 May 1891. Awarded to members of the Hazara Field Force in the Black Mountains.

"N.E. FRONTIER 1891"—28 March-7 May 1891. This clasp was awarded to the survivors of the Manipur Field Force that dealt with rebels in the state of Manipur.

"HUNZA 1891"—1-22 December 1891. This clasp was awarded to survivors of the expedition to put down rebellious natives who were firing on road-building parties. No British troops were involved.

"BURMA 1889-92"—This bar was awarded for eleven short-lived punitive expeditions that were launched for a variety of reasons.

"LUSHAI 1889-92"—11 January 1889-8 June 1892. Clasp awarded for five small expeditions into the Lushai Hills.

"CHIN HILLS 1892-93"—19 October - 10 March 1893. Awarded to the survivors of a small punitive expeditionary force against the Chins.

"KACHIN HILLS 1892-93"—3 December 1892-3 March 1893. This clasp was authorized for the survivors of a small expeditionary force into the Kachin Hills.

"WAZIRISTAN 1894-95"—22 October 1894-13 March 1895. Awarded to the members of the Waziristan Field Force for operations against the Wazirs on the Afghan border.

Medals with three or more clasps are very scarce, and while those awarded to British troops are more desirable, in many cases native troops truly bore the brunt of the fighting. ✕

Baltic Medal 1845–1855

This medal was issued almost exclusively to members of the Royal Navy and Royal Marines for operations conducted in the Baltic against Russian forces at the time of the Crimean War. However, it was also awarded to approximately one hundred members of the R. E. Sappers and Miners who were employed before Bomarsund to place demolition charges against the fortifications. The Baltic campaign included operations at Kronstadt, Kola, Bomarsund, and Petropaulovski, on the Kamtschatka Peninsula in Asia, and Sveaborg and Helsinki.

This medal was sanctioned in April 1856; was issued in silver only; and there were no clasps. The obverse of the medal bears the diademed head of young Queen Victoria and the legend "VICTORIA REGINA." The reverse of the medal shows the seated figure of Britannia looking over her left shoulder toward the fortress of Bomarsund, and holding an uplifted trident in her right hand. To her right, at a distance, is the fort at Sveaborg. In front of the rock upon which she sits is a naval cannon and a pile of cannon balls, above which are two flags with a crown between them. Above is the word "BALTIC," and in the exergue, the dates "1854-1855." The 1.25" wide ribbon is yellow with light blue edges, suspended from an ornate swiveling suspender with a claw mount sweated to the medal. The medal is usually found unnamed as issued, although members of the Royal Sappers and Miners were awarded medals impressed in the same way as the Crimean Medal of 1854-56. Many recipients had their medals inscribed at their own expense. As might be expected, medals impressed to a member of the Royal Sappers and Miners are most eagerly sought and highly valued by collectors. ⨯

Right—**Baltic Medal, 1854-55** *(Obverse)*

Far Right—**Baltic Medal, 1854-55** *(Reverse)*

Loren Schave Collection

Crimea Medal 1854–1856

This medal, of which 275,000 were awarded, commemorates the only war fought by the British against a modern European power in the period between 1815 and 1914. While well suited to Colonial warfare, this war forced the British government and the army to admit to themselves that there were many serious deficiencies, particularly in the Service of Supply and even in the quality of their generals.

The causes of the Crimean War are rather obscure, but during this period of history it was not very uncommon for nations to provide rather questionable justification for waging war. Keeping Russia out of the Bosphorus was the blunt, root cause behind this war; however, the original source of trouble was the squabble between the Greek and Latin monks in Palestine regarding which group would hold the key to the church in Bethlehem! Russia supported the Greeks, while the French and the Turks were allied behind the Latins. Seizing upon this opportunity, the Czar marched his troops into Moldavia and Wallachia, proclaiming his divine right to protect Christians there from the heathen Turks.

War was declared by Britain and France on 28 March 1854, later to be joined by the Kingdom of Sardinia. During that summer, Allied forces landed at Varna in Bulgaria. The Russians withdrew, and the Allies floundered about, searching for an elusive enemy to destroy. In September, the Allies landed an expedition in the Crimea with a view to seizing the Russian base at Sebastopol. On 20 September 1854, the Russians, entrenched on the heights above the Alma river, were attacked and defeated after a severe battle. This opened the way to the city of Sebastopol, with the British urging an immediate advance against strong opposition by the French. As a consequence, the Russians were allowed to retreat into Sebastopol, and given the respite necessary to put the entire area into a state of defense.

Following consolidation of their defense of Sebastopol, the Russians attacked Allied positions in and around Balaklava on 25 October 1854, but were driven back by determined resistance. This was the day of the glorious charge of Scarlett's Heavy Brigade, as well as the futile, but magnificent, charge of Lord Cardigan's Light Brigade.

Crimea Medal, 1854-56 *(Obverse)*

Crimea Medal, 1854-56 *(Reverse)*

Italian (Sardinian) Bersaglieri troops present in the Crimean War. Author's collection

Dead and dying after the assault on the Malakoff. Crimean War. Author's collection

British officers relaxing in camp during the Crimean War. Author's collection

Interior view after the storming of the Redan.
Author's collection

It was also outstanding in the history of the 93rd Highlanders, who fought an extremely successful engagement. Ten days later, the epic battle of Inkermann occurred. In darkness and fog, the long hours of combat involved hand-to-hand, bayonet-to-rifle-butt, and even fist-fighting, which ultimately resulted in expulsion of the Russians.

Now the siege of Sebastopol began in earnest, and the gross inefficiency of the British supply and transport system made itself deeply felt. During that winter, supply ships disgorged summer-weight uniforms, and, if stories told are to be believed, enormous shipments of boots: right-foot boots only! The greatest foes of the Allied armies were flies, fleas, fever, and frostbite, compounded by sunstroke in the summer months. Of the total 20,425 other rank fatalities in the British army, 15,894 were the result of disease! Throughout the seemingly endless ten month siege, many assaults were made on the Russian entrenchments. Then, on 8 September 1855, the Malakoff and the Redan—key positions in the Russian defens-

es—were captured by storm. The Russians retreated; set fire to the town; and sank their fleet. The war came to a virtual end.

A footnote to history: Virtually unnoticed among the Allied forces was a 10,000-man German Legion, which, after the cessation of hostilities, opted in the main to accept an offer to resettle in South Africa. In 1878, many of the original settlers, along with a number of their descendants, were recruited by Commandant Schermbrucker into the Kaffrarian Rifles in the fight against Chief Sekukuni.

The obverse of the medal bears the diademed head of young Queen Victoria, with the legend "VICTORIA REGINA 1854." The reverse bears the flying figure of Victory crowning a Roman warrior with a wreath. The warrior holds a sword in his right hand, and his left hand rests on a round shield with a lion in the center. The word "CRIMEA" is on the left of the figure. The light blue, yellow-bordered watered ribbon is attached to a foliated suspender (peculiar to this medal); the claw clasp of this suspender is sweated to the medal. Five clasps were

authorized, but no more than three will be found on a single medal. Clasps are in the shape of oak leaves with acorn ornamentation.

Clasps for Crimea Medal 1854-56 engagements:

"ALMA"
"AZOFF"—issued to the Royal Navy operating in the Sea of Azoff
"BALAKLAVA"
"INKERMANN"
"SEBASTOPOL"—anyone qualified for either "BALAKLAVA" or "INKERMANN" automatically qualified for the clasp "SEBASTOPOL."

Medals were issued unnamed, but could be returned for naming in indented capitals. Collectors prize those medals issued to the Royal Navy with clasp "AZOFF," which are extremely rare. Other highly desired named medals are those issued to the men who charged with the Light Brigade and, to a lesser extent, those issued to the Heavy Brigade. ✕

Turkish Crimea Medal 1854-1856

The Turkish Crimean Medal was issued by the Sultan of Turkey to all Allied forces engaged in the Crimean War. Three different types of medals were produced—in English, Sardinian, and French—with country destinctions denoted by the position of the flags on the obverse, and the inscription in the exergue. The British issue has a cannon, the British flag second from the right, and "Crimea 1855" in the exergue. The French issue has a cannon, the French flag second from the right, and "La Crimee 1855" in the exergue. The Sardinian issue has a cannon, the Sardinian Flag second from the right, and "La Crimea 1855" in the exergue.

Owing to the loss by shipwreck of the ship carrying the medals for the British forces, it appears that the British were indiscriminately issued whatever medals came to hand, with the Sardinian version being most commonly found.

The reverse of this medal bears the Sultan's cipher along with the Mohammedan date 1271. When originally issued, the medal was suspended by means of a ring; however, a number of recipients replaced the ring with a straight suspender of many and varied designs. The ribbon is watered crimson with green edges, with the original ribbon .50" wide. Medals were often altered in order that the normal 1.25" ribbon could be worn. Bars were never issued with this medal.

Medals were issued unnamed, although many were privately named by the recipient in a uniform manner with indented Roman letters.

While this award is almost always found along with the British Crimea Medal, a small number of British officers who had served with Turkish forces along the Danube received only the Turkish Crimea Medal. ✕

Right—**Turkish Crimea Medal** *(Obverse)*

Far Right—**Turkish Crimea Medal** *(Reverse)*

Indian Mutiny Medal 1857-1859

Trouble had been brewing in India for some time, with serious unrest developing following the annexation of the provinces of Oudh and the Punjab in 1856, which resulted in native princes fearing the loss of their thrones and territory. July 1855 had seen a revolt of the Sonthals, a northern tribe, that could not be suppressed until 1856. With the annexation of the province of Oudh in 1856, the Royal Family went to London to protest. The trip was to no avail, and the embittered prince returned to his country filled with hatred and determined to foment further trouble.

In March 1857, seven companies of the Bengal Native Infantry garrisoned at Barrackpore mutinied after a rumor circulated that they were going to be issued ammunition with cartridges that had been greased with the fat of a pig—an offense against their religion. The powder and ball were wrapped in a paper cartridge that required the cartridge to be opened by biting its end, then pouring the powder in the barrel and using the paper cartridge as wadding while the ball was rammed home. This act would defile the Sepoys, and the further rumor that they were going to be Christianized did nothing but fan the flames. The fact that the British were aware of the discontent—especially regarding the issuance of the ammunition—yet still moved ahead with plans to force the Sepoys to use the new cartridges, displayed a callous and criminal lack of understanding of the troops with whom they had long served.

Then, on 10 May of that same year, the Sepoys mutinied at Meerut—the first casualty being Colonel Finnis, the Commanding

Indian Mutiny Medal *(Obverse)*

Indian Mutiny Medal *(Reverse)*

Officer of the 11th Bengal Native Infantry. Following the Colonel's death, every white man, woman, and child in the cantonment (military establishment) was murdered in cold blood. The mutineers, joined by other rebels, then fled to Delhi and proclaimed the Great Mogul as the Emperor of India. Subsequently, they went on to besiege Cawnpore, Lucknow, and other lesser cities. When news of these events reached Governor-General Lord Canning in Calcutta,

he immediately sought help from Imperial forces.

Reinforcements slowly poured in. Naval Brigades were formed of officers and men from many of the Royal Navy ships, as well as from merchant vessels in harbor, and relief forces known as "flying columns" were dispatched in all directions to bring the mutineers under merciless attack. Delhi, already under control of the rebels, was brought under siege by British and loyal Indian

The Residency, Lucknow, March 1858. Picture Post Library

Painting of the First Relief of Lucknow. Picture Post Library

troops. Lucknow, garrisoned by a small British force and later augmented by a relief force, was besieged by the mutineers. It was not until 1858 that the siege of Lucknow and the surrounding area was lifted. The mutiny was finally quelled on 20 December, when Sir Colin Campbell, later to be Lord Clyde, announced that the last mutineer had been driven from the country.

General Order No. 363, dated 18 August 1858, and General Order No. 733 of 1859, sanctioned the Indian Mutiny Medal for all men engaged against the mutineers. General Order No. 771, of 1868, extended the medal to all those who took up arms against the rebels or who had been under fire. Two hundred ninety thousand medals were awarded.

The obverse face of the medal bears the diademed head of a young Queen Victoria with the legend "VICTORIA REGINA." On the reverse is a standing helmeted figure of Britannia holding a wreath in her outstretched right hand, with the Union Shield over her left arm. Behind Britannia is the British Lion and above is the word "INDIA." In the exergue are the dates "1857-1858." The 1.25" ribbon, which is white with two .25" red stripes (popularly believed to represent red for the blood shed, and white for the slaughtered innocents), is suspended from a very unusual horn-shaped suspender attached to the medal by a high swiveling claw. The recipient's name and regiment are indented on the rim of the medal in Roman letters.

There are five clasps possible for this medal; however, no medal bears more than four, and there were less than two hundred of these. The bars are fish-tailed, and separated from the suspender and each other by rosettes. Clasps should be read from top to bottom. The clasps include:

"DELHI"—30 May-14 September 1857. Awarded to those troops employed in the recapture of the city. Due to death and illness, there were four different commanders of this force between 14 May and 14 September 1857.

"DEFENCE OF LUCKNOW"—29 June-22 November 1857. Awarded to the original defense force (1,698) and to the relief force commanded by Sir Henry Havelock (2,716).

"RELIEF OF LUCKNOW"—November 1857. This clasp was awarded to troops under the command of Sir Colin Campbell who were engaged in the relief of the city.

"LUCKNOW"—November 1857-March 1858. Awarded to those troops under Sir Colin Campbell who took part in final operations that resulted in the surrender of the city and the clearing of the surrounding areas.

"CENTRAL INDIA"—January-June, 1858. Awarded to all those who served in the forces under Major-General Sir Hugh Rose against Jhansi, Calpee, and Gwalior, as well as all those who had served in the Rajpatana Field Force and the Madras Column between January and June, 1858. ✕

Second China War Medal 1857-1860

Events leading to what is now known as the Second China War were supposedly similar to those that led to the First China War—ostensibly, maltreatment of Europeans. However, this was mainly an excuse to corner more of the lucrative Chinese market, especially the opium trade.

Chinese authorities in Canton boarded the ship "ARROW," sailing under British colors; removed twelve of her crew; and hauled down the ship's flag. British naval authorities demanded redress, but none was forthcoming from the Chinese.

On 23 October 1856, British troops seized the Barrier forts and then entered the city of Canton. Understaffed, an appeal was made for reinforcements, which were agonizingly slow in materializing due to the heavy demand for troops needed elsewhere to put down the Indian Mutiny. However, by March 1857, sufficient forces finally arrived. In May, the Chinese fleet in Escape Creek was destroyed by British Naval Forces, and another attack on the Chinese fleet in Fatshan Creek yielded the same results. After a further delay, Canton was besieged and finally captured in early 1858.

Far to the north in the Gulf of Pechili, a joint British-French Naval Force attacked the Taku Forts in May 1858. The forts surrendered after a severe pasting by British Armstrong breech-loading rifled cannons. Hoping to gain time to re-equip, the Chinese signed a peace treaty; however, neither signatory really trusted the other! The treaty stipulated that Britain and France would be represented by ambassadors at the Imperial Court in Pekin. However, the ambassador, on his way to Pekin, was fired on by the Taku Forts. After an unsuccessful attempt to take the forts, the British and French were forced into a full-scale operation involving the landing of some 13,000 European and Indian troops, bolstered by a further contingent of 6,700 French troops.

Operations were commenced in August 1860, with the capture of the Taku Forts on the 21st. The Chinese attempted to stall at Tientsin, but the combined forces pushed on to the capital at Pekin, which was entered on 13 October after two engagements at Chiang-kia-wan, on 18 September, and Pa-li-chian, on 21 September. Another peace treaty was signed on 24 October, with Pekin evacuated by the Allies on 5 November. As a footnote, the Summer Palace in Pekin was burned to the ground by British troops after it had been thoroughly looted by the French.

Second China War Medal *(Obverse)*

Second China War Medal *(Reverse)*

Taku forts, revealing the destruction inflicted by the bombardment.
Wupperfeld collection

The Second China War Medal was awarded to all Naval and Military personnel engaged during the period 25 May 1857 to 13 October 1860. There were six clasps authorized for this medal; however, the most awarded were five to a single man.

The obverse of the medal bears the diademed head of young Queen Victoria with the legend "VICTORIA REGINA." The reverse bears an oval shield with Royal Arms in the center against a collection of war trophies, all in front of a palm tree. Above is inscribed "ARMIS EXPOSCERE PACEM." In the exergue is the word "CHINA." A horn-shaped suspender, similar to that used on the Indian Mutiny Medal, is attached by means of a high, swiveling claw sweated to the medal. The original 1.25" wide ribbon issued with the medal was multicolored, with five equally spaced stripes of blue, yellow, red, white, and green. The ribbon later adopted is crimson with yellow edges.

Clasps for this medal are as follows:

"CHINA 1842"—93 awarded. This bar was to be awarded to those of Her Majesty's forces who had already received the "CHINA 1842" Medal and had also served in the operations from 1857-1860.

"FATSHAN 1857"—This bar was awarded only to Naval and Marine personnel from H. M. ships involved in that particular operation.

"CANTON 1857"—Awarded to those regiments and the Naval Brigade present at this action.

"TAKU FORTS 1858"—Awarded only to those Naval and Marine personnel from H. M. ships present at the action.

"TAKU FORTS 1860"—Awarded to regiments and Naval personnel from ships involved in this operation. Indian marine ships were also part of the combined forces.

"PEKIN 1860"—Awarded to regiments, Royal Naval, and Royal Indian Marine personnel present at this engagement.

Awards to the Royal Navy were not named, but those presented to soldiers and marines were named in indented Roman capitals. Medals named to members of the 1st Dragoon Guards, the only cavalry unit present, are highly sought after by collectors, as are medals awarded to the Indian Marine, which are very rare.

No. 2051, John Moyse, a private of "The Buffs," was captured by Tartar cavalry. When brought before the local mandarin, he refused to bow before a "Chinese 'eathen" and he was beheaded as a result! This earned John Moyse a front page story in the *Times*; a place in the Buffs Regimental history; and immortality in a poem by Sir Francis Doyle—a rather prime example of Victorian sentiment! ✕

New Zealand Medal 1845-47 and 1860-66

The outbreak of war in the beautiful islands of New Zealand was caused by the gradual encroachment of the white man, who was taking more land from the native Maoris than signed treaties called for, and always at a figure that favored the Europeans. The result was that the natives rose in rebellion in 1845, leading to much bush fighting—at which the natives excelled—with the conflict gradually being brought under control in the North Island in 1846, and in the South Island in 1847.

In 1860, the Maoris again rose in revolt after having been cheated out of more land by the government. Formerly peaceful natives reacted to the revolt with great enthusiasm, causing the authorities to dispatch troops from as far away as Great Britain, Burma, and India to help quell the uprising. After a nasty defeat of the Maoris at Mahoetahi on 6 November 1860, a treaty was signed and peace was finally restored in March, 1861.

On 4 May 1863, fighting flared anew and rapidly spread across the islands, with more troops being sent in on demand. Some of these troops landed and encamped on a narrow peninsula called Te-pap. Exercising extreme stupidity, the British had allowed the Maoris to build a high wooden stockade, called a "pah," which consisted of two parallel wooden stockade walls with the space between filled with earth, and which stretched across the entire peninsula, thereby very effectively blocking the exit of the British! This was known as the gate to the interior by the British, and was referred to as the Gate Pah. The blockade was attacked on 28 April 1864. Since the pah

New Zealand Medal *(Obverse)*

New Zealand Medal *(Reverse)*

was virtually impervious to gunfire, the British troops became confused, and the ensuing panic led to their defeat at day's end.

The war continued in the way colonial wars so often did: Peace was finally declared 3 July 1866, even though disturbances continued through 1881! British troops were withdrawn from the islands of New Zealand in January 1870.

In 1869, this medal was finally awarded to the survivors of those who had fought in both the Maori War of 1845-47 and the continuation war of 1860-66. The medal was issued to naval and military personnel, and to the local militia

forces as well. The New Zealand medal rates as one of the most confusing campaign medals ever issued, with twenty-nine different reverse types having been made, twenty-eight of which bear dates, with one remaining undated. Most awards to the Army are undated, while the three hundred or so medals awarded to members of the Royal Navy are appropriately dated on the reverse.

The obverse of the medal bears the diademed head of Victoria with a veil covering the back of her head, around which is the legend "VICTORIA D: G: BRITT: REG: F: D:". In the center of the reverse, surrounded by a laurel wreath, is the date or dates of service; above are the words "NEW ZEALAND" and below "VIRTUTIS HONOR." The design of a straight, swiveling, foliated suspender was used exclusively for this medal. The 1.25" wide ribbon is dark blue with a .375" wide red stripe down the center. Generally the medal is impressed with neat Roman capitals when awarded to Army or Navy personnel, while some awards to local militias are found engraved.

Medals will be found with any of the following dates: 1845-46; 1845-47; 1846-47; 1846; 1847; 1848; 1860; 1860-61; 1860-63; 1860-64; 1860-65; 1860-66; 1861; 1861-63; 1861-64; 1861-65; 1861-66; 1862-66; 1863; 1863-64; 1863-65; 1863-66; 1864; 1864-65; 1864-66; 1865; 1865-66; and 1866.

Collectors are most eager to find medals named to individuals engaged in the battle of the Gate Pah, as this was an example of British troops breaking in battle with well-armed natives. ×

Canadian General Service Medal 1866-1870

Thirty-three years after the fact, approval was given to the Canadian Government to issue a medal to all survivors of those Imperial or Canadian Militia Forces that had taken part in suppression of the Irish Fenian raids and Louis Riel's First Rebellion. Approximately 17,600 medals were issued, with about 15,300 going to Canadian Militia units.

As early as 1837, a local politician, Louis J. Papineau, was trying to arouse his followers to rebellion and, he hoped, separation of Canada from Great Britain. Activities such as this made the Canadian authorities realize that their militia forces would have to be more efficiently organized.

The potato famine and the lure of a country rife with opportunities had brought literally hundreds of thousands of Irish to the United States and Canada. A large number of these men were members of the Irish Fenian Brotherhood, sworn to separate Ireland from the stranglehold of Great Britain. Many had fought for the Union during the Civil War in the United States, and had thereby gained valuable battlefield experience. On 31 May 1866, semi-organized and led by Colonel John O'Neill, a large force of Irish soldiers-of-fortune assembled on the Niagara River and proceeded to invade Canada. In this, their first engagement, the makeshift "army" defeated a unit of Canadian Militia, but elected to hastily retire across the border after having been told that a large force was on its way to attack them. To their great surprise, they were arrested by U.S. authorities on arrival in the States, and so ended the First Fenian Raid!

In January, 1870, Louis Riel, a French-Canadian firebrand, seized Fort Garry in the Hudson Bay Territory (including the Hudson Bay Company's treasury), and he launched a rebellion. Acting on the assumption that this would be a good time to once again invade Canada, O'Neill crossed the border with his men yet another time, only to be quickly turned back and re-arrested by U.S. authorities.

An expedition was quickly dispatched to recapture Fort Garry. Upon arrival at the fort, the column discovered that Riel and his followers had already fled—to be heard from once again some fifteen years later!

On the obverse of the medal appears the diademed, veiled bust of Queen Victoria, wearing the Ribbon and the Star of the Garter, with a small Imperial crown placed above the veil, atop which the legend "VICTORIA REGINA ET IMPERATRIX" appears. The reverse bears the Canadian flag between two branches of maple leaves; above is the word "CANADA." The suspender is a straight bar, with a claw attachment fixed by a rivet. The 1.25" ribbon is scarlet with a white stripe down the middle. Names of the recipient are indented and engraved around the edge of the medal.

Three bars were issued, as follows:

"FENIAN RAID 1866"

"FENIAN RAID 1870"

"RED RIVER 1870"

No medal was issued without a bar, but only twenty medals carried all three bars. ✕

Far Left—**Canadian General Service Medal (Obverse)**

Left—**Canadian General Service Medal (Reverse)**

Abyssinian War Medal
4 October 1867–19 April 1868

The Abyssinian War resulted from a strange "hobby" of Abyssinia's King, Theodore, who delighted in throwing people, including the British Consul, missionaries, and other British subjects, into prison for the pure joy of it! Negotiators worked for a year to secure their release, only to have the entire group—which included the negotiators themselves—thrown into prison one month later. Ultimatums and formal letters flew back and forth, with the Queen finally declaring war on 19 November 1867.

On 18 January 1868, troops were landed at Massawah and the strength of the force was built up. When sufficient numbers were available, the three-hundred-plus-mile trek to Magdala started. The battle of Arrogie was fought on 10 April, with Magdala, the capital, falling on the 13th. The Royal Navy had supplied a brigade of eighty-three men outfitted with twelve-pounder Congreve rocket tubes. These rockets so unnerved the Abyssinians that they fled from the fortress. In the meantime, the King had committed suicide. However, neither of these events deterred the British, who proceeded to raze the capital to the ground before commencing their return journey.

This was undoubtedly one of the most—if not the most—bloodless campaigns ever fought by the British, and the casualty count amounted to two killed and twenty-seven wounded. Thirty-seven other men succumbed to disease. This medal is a disappointment to collectors who enjoy a "bloody" history with their medals!

Abyssinian War Medal *(Obverse)*

Abyssinian War Medal *(Reverse)*

Approximately 14,000 medals were issued, with about 2,000 of that number awarded to the Royal Navy. Naval awards were made to all personnel of naval vessels on duty in the Red Sea, as well as to any member of the Service who had anything whatsoever to do with the war. This medal proved to be one of the most expensive general issue medals ever produced by the British, as each recipient's name was embossed on the medal, necessitating a separate die for each.

The obverse of the medal bears the small veiled bust of Queen Victoria with coronet, surrounded by a nine-pointed star, between each point of which is one of the

Rocket batteries in action outside the fortress of Magdala.
Author's collection

letters of the word "ABYSSINIA." The reverse bears the embossed name of the recipient along with the name of his regiment or ship within a laurel wreath. The 1.50" wide ribbon is white, with a broad red stripe running down the center. The medal is suspended from this ribbon by means of a silver ring attached to a crown sweated to the medal. As stated, naming was by embossing; however, some medals awarded to native troops were named by engraving. There were no bars for this medal. ✕

Ashantee War Medal
9 June 1873–4 February 1874

In Ghana—or the Gold Coast, as it was formerly known—the port of Elmina was originally founded by the Portuguese and then captured by the Dutch in 1637. The Dutch subsequently ceded the port to the British, very much to the consternation of King Kalkali, or "King Coffee," as he was known. The King had been receiving a small sum from the Dutch for their use of the port. However, the British felt this was an unnecessary expenditure. The King was annoyed at such arrogance and promptly attacked the friendly natives around the port area, causing much nastiness.

A situation such as this could not be allowed to continue, so while Major-General Sir Garnet Wolseley was preparing a proper force to deal with the restless natives, a small naval brigade commenced operations against King Kalkali, shelling the town of Chamah. This was the first phase of the operation. Troops arrived on 17 December 1873, and the advance on Coomassie, the capital, was begun on 5 January 1874. Several major engagements were fought, with the advance hampered somewhat by the terrain and resistance from the Ashanti. Coomassie was reached early in February 1874 , with peace being effected on 13 February. This was another campaign in which casualties were extremely light, with more men down from disease than from wounds.

This medal was awarded in silver to combatant troops, and in bronze to local transport personnel (extremely rare, and quite difficult to find!). The obverse of the medal bears the diademed head of Queen Victoria with veil, with the legend "VICTORIA REGINA." The reverse of the medal is comprised of scenes representing the British fighting the natives in the brush, with a body depicted in the foreground, and branches everywhere. The 1.25" wide yellow ribbon with black borders and two thin black stripes down the middle is suspended from a straight suspender that is sweated to the medal. Naming of the recipient is in indented Roman capitals with the date "1873-74," with the lettering filled-in in black.

There was one bar issued inscribed "COOMASSIE" and it was awarded to all those who crossed the River Prah and to those who took place in the actions at Amoaful and Ardahsa on 31 January and 4 February, respectively. Royal Navy personnel received approximately 3,500 medals for their actions. ✕

Ashantee War Medal *(Obverse)*

Ashantee War Medal *(Reverse)*

Troops disembarking on the Gold Coast. The Ashanti War, 1873-74. Wupperfeld collection

South African War Medal
Zulu and Basuto Wars
25 September 1877–2 December 1879

In 1877, natives friendly to the British were attacked by dissident enemy tribes. This required the British to punish the offenders and a field force was formed and dispatched to rout the malefactors. This campaign, known as the Gaika-Galeka War, also involved many local militia and volunteer units. Colonial units alone fought against Chief Pokwane and Griqua tribes in Griqualand West near Kimberley during 1878.

In September of 1878, King Cetewayo created an incident by refusing to release prisoners captured during a raid. Refusing response to a British ultimatum, Cetewayo set into motion a retaliatory British force of five columns which then crossed the border into Zululand on 11 January 1879. Four of the columns spread out in their advance, while the fifth remained near the border at Isandhlwana. It was here that the British, completely unprepared, were attacked and decimated by Dambulamanzi, Cetewayo's half-brother. While some troops managed to escape, 1,329 men, including native levies, were slaughtered. Flushed with success, on that very night the Zulu regiments, comprised of more than 3,000 men, attacked a small garrison of one hundred and thirty nine men at Rorke's Drift on the Tugela River. This attack produced a spectacular defense and final repulse of the Zulu tribes which earned the garrison, under the command of Lieutenants Bromhead and Chard, eleven Victoria Crosses.

Meanwhile, additional engagements were taking place between Zulu forces and the other columns that had entered Zululand. Colonel Pearson found himself surrounded at Eshowe, while Colonel Wood found it necessary to fall back to Kambula. It was not until after the Zulu defeat at Gingindhlovu that Colonel Pearson's troops were relieved. Meantime, Colonel Wood had defeated Zulu forces in the Zlobani mountains on 28 March, and again the next day defeated them at Kambula. Further reinforcements were dispatched from England, which aided in the defeat of Cetewayo at the battle of Ulundi. On 1 September, the Zulu War was declared over.

However, while these actions against the Zulu tribes were in progress, yet another campaign was being fought against dissidents operating in the northeast corner of the Transvaal. That campaign ended on 2 December 1879. Another Basuto Chief, Moirosi, refused to pay his taxes and had fled to the Drakensberg

South African War Medal *(Obverse)*

South African War Medal *(Reverse)*

The Last Stand at Isandhlwana. *The Graphic,* 15 March 1879

The Mission Station at Rorke's Drift after the battle, showing only the storehouse and cattle kraal still standing. Wupperfeld collection

Mountains, where he and all his followers were eventually hunted down and killed. From the British point of view, this was certainly justifiable punishment for refusing to give the tax man his due!

Sanctioned in 1880, this medal is exactly the same as the medal instituted for the previous South African campaigns between 1834 and 1853, except that the date on the reverse of the more recent medal has been replaced by a shield and four crossed assegais. The obverse of the medal bears the diademed head of Queen Victoria above which is the legend "VICTORIA REGINA." The reverse shows a lion crouching beside a mimosa bush, with the words "SOUTH AFRICA" above and the revised exergue below. The 1.25" ribbon is yellow-orange, with two broad and two

narrow blue stripes. Suspension is by means of an ornate scroll suspender and claw mount which has been sweated onto the medal. Naming is almost always done in engraved capitals, either upright or sloping.

The medal will be found without a clasp, or with the clasps described below. ×

Authorized clasps:

"1877"—This clasp is uncommon and highly collectible.

"1877-8"—Scarce clasp

"1877-8-9"

"1878"

"1878-9"—Scarce clasp

"1879"—Most common of the clasps issued.

The Last of the 24th - Isandhlwana.
Painting by R. T. Moynan

The end of the battle of Kambula, with the Zulus being driven back into the ravine. By Orlando Norie

Afghanistan Medal 1878–1880

During the entire period of India's occupation by the British, one of the greatest fears related to southward expansion undertaken by the Russians—be they Czar or Commissar—and this constantly involved the threat of Russian meddling in the affairs of Afghanistan.

Matters got off to a bad start in 1878 when Shere Ali, the ruler of Afghanistan, signed a treaty with Russia and refused to allow the British to maintain a Resident in Kabul. The British could not abide such an affront, so an ultimatum was sent to the Afghans and it was totally ignored. In November of 1878 the British, now goaded beyond endurance at the insults received, immediately dispatched three previously formed columns of troops into Afghanistan.

The Afghans were defeated at the battles of Musjid and Peiwar Khotal. The British advanced, and the Afghans sued for peace—a peace under which the British were allowed to dictate Afghanistan's foreign policy in return for British protection. In consideration of a sizeable annuity granted by the British, the Amir of Afghanistan allowed the British to dispatch a Major Cavagnari as the Resident in Kabul. Wily as always, the Afghans massacred the Major and his party in September 1879, and the war heated-up once again!

Afghanistan, 1878-1880 *(Obverse)*

Afghanistan, 1878-1880 *(Reverse)*

Fort of Ali Musjid, Khyber Pass. Captured by Lt. General Samuel Browne.
Author's collection

There was to be considerably more fighting in the second phase of the war than in the first, with the Kabul Field Force, under Roberts, working its way into Afghanistan to Charasia, south-west of the city of Kabul. Here Roberts defeated the enemy with the loss of only eighteen killed and seventy wounded. The city of Kabul was Roberts' and the occupation was swift. Cordially hated, the British found enemy forces advancing on the city, and this forced Roberts to withdraw into defensive positions in Sherpur, while the enemy occupied Kabul and its fortress, Bala Hissar. The Afghans were beaten off and the opposition finally melted away by the end of December 1879. On 30 March 1880, Sir Donald Stewart

Typical fort on the Indian Frontier, c. 1880. Wupperfeld collection

British garrison on parade in Kabul, Afghanistan. Wupperfeld collection

Saving the guns at Maiwand 27 July 1880. Print by R. Caton Woodville

92nd Highlanders in action at Kandahar, 1 Sept. 1880.
R. Caton Woodville

Fortress of Upper Bala Hissar from the gateway above the British Residency, Kabul. Author's collection

moved his force from Kandahar to Kabul, leaving behind a garrison charged with protecting the former city. Stewart engaged the enemy on 19 April, and reached Kabul in May.

In August, word was received that a British brigade had been nearly annihilated at Maiwand—the Horse Artillery and the 66th Foot suffering terribly. Elsewhere, the garrison at Kandahar came under heavy pressure, and General Roberts was dispatched to lift the siege, resulting in the famous "march from Kabul to Kandahar." On the approach of the relief column, the enemy lifted their siege of the city and took to entrenchments in the surrounding areas. On 1 September, after resting his troops, Roberts attacked the Afghan positions, completely routing the enemy and capturing all of their guns.

The British now withdrew their forces from the country, having proven that while they could take Afghanistan in battle, they could not hold the country. . . a bitter lesson the Russians would learn a century later. Except for the military honors garnered by the British forces, nothing had really been attained.

This medal was authorized 19 March 1881. The obverse showed the crowned, veiled bust of Queen Victoria, adorned with earrings, necklace and pendant, and wearing the Ribbon and Star of the Order of the Garter. The bust is surrounded by the legend "VICTORIA REGINA ET IMPERATRIX." The reverse shows Anglo-Indian troops on the march, with an officer riding in the foreground. In the center is an elephant carrying a mountain gun, while in the background is a mountain-top fortress. The word "AFGHANISTAN" is shown above, while in the exergue is the date "1878-79-80." The 1.25" wide ribbon is green and has red edges. The medal is suspended by a straight, plain silver bar with claw clip attachment riveted to the medal. The name and regiment of the recipient is engraved along the edge in capital letters.

Six clasps were authorized for this medal, but only four could be earned by any one man. ✕

Authorized clasps are:
"ALI MUSJID"—21 November 1878
"PEIWAR KOTAL"—2 December 1878
"CHARASIA"—6 October 1879
"KABUL"—10-23 December 1879
"AHMED KHEL"—19 April 1880
"KANDAHAR"—1 September 1880

Kabul to Khandahar Star
9–31 August 1880

This medal was awarded to all those—European and Indian—who took part in Lord Roberts' famous August 1880 march from Kabul to relieve the siege on Khandahar. Roberts' force departed Kabul and marched some three hundred and ten miles through terrible Afghan terrain to relieve the garrison. This medal could only be awarded to those who qualified for the Afghanistan Medal (bar "Khandahar") of 1878-80.

The medal is made from the bronze of captured Afghani guns at the battle of Khandahar. The obverse is a five-pointed star with a ball between all of the points except the top two. In the center is the raised monogram "V.R.I." surrounded by a raised circular border on which appears, in raised lettering, "KABUL TO KHANDAHAR," with the date "1880" in the center at the bottom. Topping the star is a crown to which the ring for the suspension is attached.

The reverse of the medal is plain except for the naming of the recipient around the hollow center, with indented capital letters for the British and engraved capitals or sloping script for the Indian troops. An interesting side note is that frequently with named medals, the term "Foot" is used instead of "Regt." up until the reforms of 1881. The ribbon is the familiar India rainbow pattern of red, white, yellow, white, and blue. There were no bars issued for this medal.

Awards were presented to: one British cavalry regiment; three Indian cavalry regiments; three batteries of artillery; four British infantry regiments; ten Indian infantry regiments; plus the usual ancillary forces.

Collectors are advised to carefully examine any of these medals offered for sale, as numerous well-made copies have surfaced over the years. ✕

Kabul to Khandahur Star *(Obverse)*

Want to Fight for England.

Want to Fight for England.

Cape of Good Hope General Service Medal 1880-1897

General unrest and small uprisings in the Cape Colony during the period 1880-1897 necessitated sending out small expeditionary forces to put down local troubles. After the defeat of their chief, Moirosi, the Basutos were ordered to turn in their firearms and all other weapons. This order was resisted by Chief Lerothodi and his people, who then waged war on the colonists. Defeated by the British in separate battles at Mafetang and then at Kalabani in 1880, the Basutos were again defeated at Tweefontein in 1881. A peace agreement was reached in April of 1881.

A very serious cattle disease in 1896 necessitated the destruction of huge herds of native cattle, a move which was fiercely resisted by the population, and which resulted in much fighting before order was finally restored to the colonies. It is interesting to note that of 5,250 medals awarded, only fifteen were to British soldiers, with the rest of the awards going to colonial troops.

This medal, in silver only, was issued by the Cape Government in 1900 with the approval of the Crown. The obverse of the medal bears the bust of Queen Victoria, crowned and veiled, wearing the earrings, necklace and pendant, as well as the Ribbon and Star of the Garter. The bust is surrounded by the legend "VICTORIA REGINA ET IMPERATRIX."

The reverse bears the arms of the Cape Colony with, above on a raised border, "CAPE OF GOOD HOPE." Below, on a scroll, is "SPES CONA" and a fir-cone with foliage. The 1.25" ribbon comprises equal vertical bands of dark blue, orange, and dark blue, from which the medal is suspended by a straight suspender bar with an ornamental clip attached to the medal by a rivet. Naming of the recipient is in faint, indented, as well as engraved, block capitals.

Three clasps were authorized for this medal, and, according to

Far Left—**Cape of Good Hope General Service Medal** (*Obverse*)

Left—**Cape of Good Hope General Service Medal** (*Reverse*)

records, only ten medals were issued without bars. The clasps are as follows, with the number awarded shown in brackets:

"TRANSKEI" [1,070]—13 September 1880-13 May 1881. This bar was for operations in Tembuland and Griqualand East, where the natives refused to hand in their firearms. Action covered by the clasp overlaps that for which the following clasp was awarded.

"BASUTOLAND" [2,150]—13 September 1880-27 April 1881. As a result of nearly continuous sporadic fighting, Basutoland became a Crown Colony in March 1884.

"BECHUANALAND" [2,580]—24 December 1896-30 July 1897. This clasp was awarded for the supression of a native revolt.

Only twenty-three medals were issued with all three clasps, and medals with but two clasps are considered quite rare and highly collectible. ✕

Egypt 1882-1889

28

Protecting and keeping open the Suez Canal was of paramount importance to the British during their long reign in the Middle and Far East, for the lifelines of the Empire depended upon easy access through the Mediterranean to the canal and, from there, to Britain's far-flung outposts.

The corrupt Khedive of Egypt, Mehmit Ali, was forced to sell his shares in the Suez Canal to Great Britain. Soon thereafter he was replaced by his even more notoriously corrupt son, Tewfik. For the long-unpaid Egyptian army, this was the last straw, and it led to mutiny under the hand of Arabi Pasha, Egyptian Minister of War—the Abdul Gamal Nasser of his day. Arabi began in earnest to build and strengthen the defenses of Alexandria, and threatened to sieze the Suez Canal. The British, ever vigilant to threats to its life-lines, could not allow this to happen. After issuing a firm ultimatum, the British fleet bombarded Alexandria, and landed troops to "restore order!"

Finding the Egyptian army entrenched at Tel-el-Kebir, the British undertook a night march and routed the Egyptians. British forces remained in Egypt to protect the Suez Canal. Both combined to thus end the first phase of the Egyptian campaign.

Great Britain now found itself with the responsibility for a country in chaos, without leadership, administration, or an army. At this propitious moment the "Mahdi," or "expected one"—a religious fanatic—appeared in the Sudan, a region nominally under control of

Egypt, 1882-1889, with bar "Gemaizah 1888" *(Obverse)*

Egypt, 1882-1889 *(Reverse)*

Egypt, and commenced fanning the flames of religious rebellion. An Egyptian army of 10,000 under the command of a British officer, Hicks Pasha, was dispatched to quell the rebellion, but to the last man all were slaughtered by the Mahdists. Their weapons, guns, and almost one million rounds of

ammunition fell into the hands of the rebels. The British advanced on the rebels from the coast and, after victories at El-Teb and Tamaai, withdrew once again to the coast.

The British then totally withdrew from the Sudan, leaving "Chinese" Gordon to manage the

British soldiers on the Egyptian Campaign, 1882, illustrating home-service uniforms used by the troops. Wupperfeld collection

Egyptian army at Alexandria, c. 1882, with a modern Krupps breech-loading field gun. Wupperfeld collection

Inside the square of the 1st Black Watch and the 1st Yorks and Lancaster at Tamaai. From a painting by G. D. Giles

The Black Watch attacking under fire at Tel-El-Kebir. Wupperfeld collection

The 2nd Bn., Royal Irish Regiment smashing the Egyptian defenses at Tel-El-Kebir. Wupperfeld collection

Celebrating the capture of Tel-El-Kebir, Egypt, 1882. Wupperfeld collection

evacuation of the garrisons and civil staff. But, at the end of 1884 Gordon found himself and his charges under siege in Khartoum. Belatedly, a relief column fought its way into Khartoum forty-eight hours too late to prevent the fall of the city and the murder of Gordon. At about the same time, new battles erupted in the Sudan, and the British once more withdrew. However, fighting continued along the frontier, including battles at Gemaizah and Toski.

The obverse of the medal bears the diademed head of Queen Victoria and the legend "VICTORIA REGINA ET IMPERATRIX." The reverse bears a depiction of the Sphinx atop a pedestal, with "EGYPT" above. In the exergue the date "1882" appears for those medals awarded in the first campaign; those

Egypt, 1882-1889, with bars "El Teb-Tamaai," "The Nile 1884-85," and "Kirbekan."

New South Wales contingent on the march in the Sudan, 1885. From an engraving by Charles E. Fripp

awarded later have a plain exergue. The 1.25" wide ribbon has three bright blue and two white stripes of equal width, from which the medal is suspended by a straight swiveling suspender. Dated medals were engraved in sloping capital letters, while the undated medals are impressed in sloping capitals, excluding those which were awarded to Royal Marines which are impressed in large, bold, and upright capitals. Those medals awarded to Indian troops are named in neat, small, running script, while the medals awarded to Egyptian troops are named in Arabic.

A total of thirteen clasps were authorized for this medal. The maximum number of clasps on a medal is seven—only one was awarded. Six medals were issued with six clasps, while those with five clasps are also very rare. The clasp "ABU KLEA" as well as the clasp "KIRBEKAN" must be accompanied by the clasp "THE NILE 1884-5;" and "TOFREK" must accompany "SUAKIN 1885." ✕

Authorized clasps for the Egypt, 1882-1889 Medal:

"ALEXANDRIA"—11 July 1882. Given for the bombardment of Alexandria by the ships under Admiral Seymour.

"TEL-EL-KEBIR"—13 September 1882

"EL-TEB"—29 February 1884

"TAMAAI"—13 March 1884. Also spelled "Tamaii" in official records.

"EL-TEB-TAMAAI"—Awarded to those who took part in both actions.

"SUAKIN 1884"

"THE NILE 1884-85"—Awarded those who took part in the column to relieve Gordon.

"ABU KLEA"—17 January 1885. A terrible engagement wherein a British square was broken for the only time in recorded memory.

"KIRBEKAN"—In conjunction with the preceding clasp, this clasp is always found with "THE NILE 1884-85" clasp.

"SUAKIN 1885"

"TOFREK"—This clasp is always found in conjunction with the preceding clasp.

"GEMAIZAH"—20 December 1888

"TOSKI"—3 August 1889

The Khedive's Star
1882-1891

These five-pointed, all-bronze stars were awarded to those who also received the Egypt Medal of 1882-89. Produced in Birmingham, England, by Messrs. Henry Jenkins and Sons, the medal was struck on order of the Khedive, Tewfik Mahommed.

The obverse of the medal depicts the Sphinx, with three pyramids behind. Around this is a raised circle on which is embossed the word "EGYPT," followed by the applicable date or dates. There were four issues of these medals, corresponding with the different campaigns. The first three issues bear the date on the obverse, while the fourth is undated. The fourth issue has the word "EGYPT" in the center at the top of the circle. The reverse of the medal bears the Khedive's monogram "T.M." within a raised circle. A small ring is attached to the medal between two points of the star; a straight suspender, in the middle of which is the crescent and a five-pointed star, is attached to the ring. The medal is suspended from a plain blue 1.50" wide ribbon. There was one bar for "TOKAR" issued with this medal.

The relevant dated medals are as follows:

- Star dated "1882" for the campaign between 16 July and 14 September 1882.
- Star dated "1884" for the campaign between 19 February and 26 March 1884.
- Star dated "1884-6" for the campaigns between 26 March 1884 and 7 October 1886.

The Khedive's Star, 1882-1891 *(Obverse)*

The Khedive's Star *(Reverse)*

- Star undated for the campaigns between 26 March 1884 and 7 October 1886.

Only one star per member was issued. The Khedive made a further issue of undated stars to commemorate the action at Tokar on 19 February 1891. Those present at the action who had not already received a star were awarded one with the bar "TOKAR 1308H" in Arabic. Previous star recipients received the bar only. By the time the last star was awarded, there were very few men who had not already received an earlier one, so an undated star with the bar "TOKAR" is quite rare. ✕

North West Canada 1885

L ouis Riel had escaped from Fort Garry when the facility was captured after the Red River Campaign of 1870. When the Canadian government decided, in 1885, to open up the great North West Territories, Riel saw this as yet another opportunity to raise the flag of rebellion. Rallying the local Indians to his cause, he boldly proclaimed himself leader of a provisional government, promising just about everything and anything to those who would join the movement.

Reacting quickly to this new threat, the Canadian government mobilized almost the entire force available and quickly moved to quench the fires of rebellion by moving the militia over the newly completed network of railroads. In a campaign which lasted from 24 April to 28 May 1885, General Middleton completely routed the rebels, and Louis Riel was captured. After a swift trial, he was hung, and the rebellious problems ended with his death.

The obverse of the medal bears the veiled, diademed head of Queen Victoria surrounded by the words "VICTORIA REGINA ET IMPERATRIX." The reverse face bears the legend "NORTH WEST CANADA" and the date "1885" surrounded by a wreath of maple leaves. The medal hangs from a 1.25" wide blue-gray ribbon with two red stripes which almost touch the edges, and is hung by means of a straight suspender with claw mount sweated to the medal. There was only one clasp for "SASKATCHEWAN" awarded with this medal (approximately 1,760 awarded) to all those who had taken part in any or all of the three main skirmishes during the rebellion. With the exception of sixteen British officers on staff at that time, no British troops were involved. The medals were issued unnamed, but many were locally impressed, generally in an abbreviated manner. ✕

Far Left—**North West Canada, 1885** *(Obverse)*

Left—**North West Canada** *(Reverse)*

While slightly thinner, this medal is identical, down to the suspension and the ribbon, to the one awarded for the Ashantee Campaign of 1873-74. Those who had earlier received the Ashantee Medal, either with or without the bar "COOMASSIE," were only awarded the appropriate bar or bars for further service in East and West Africa between the years 1887 and 1900. Those men who had not received the Ashantee medal received the East and West Africa Medal.

Consequently, the only way to determine if a man had been in the Ashantee War but had not received the bar for "COOMASSIE" is to compare the thickness of the two medals. Twenty-three bars were finally authorized but, for reasons unknown, the M'wele campaign in 1895-6 failed to qualify for a bar although the name and date was engraved around the rim of the medal! The greatest number of bars seen on this medal is seven; however, there may be medals with more than this number. Medals were issued in silver, although a few awarded to native troops were made in bronze. Medals are named in sloping script.

The following bars were authorized for this medal:

"1887-8"—13 November 1887-2 January 1888. Awarded for operations against the Tonnie Tribe.

"WITU 1890"—17-27 October 1890. Issued to participants in a punitive expedition against the Sultan of Witu.

"1891-2"—29 December 1891-2 February 1892. Awarded to troops taking part in an expedition to Gambia.

East and West Africa Medal, 1887-1900 *(Obverse)*

East and West Africa Medal *(Reverse)*

"1892"—8 March-25 May 1892. Issued to troops taking part in the expeditions against Tambi, Toniataba, and the Jebus.

"WITU AUGUST 1893"—7-13 August 1893. Received by those troops involved in putting down further trouble with the Sultan of Witu.

"LIWONDI 1893"—February-March 1893. Recipients were members of a small naval force sent against Chief Liwondi.

"JUBA RIVER 1893"—23-25 August 1893. Awarded to those involved in a small volunteer force in action against the Somalis.

"LAKE NYASSA 1893"—November 1893. Accorded to those members of a small volunteer boat party in action against a local tribal chief.

"1893-94"—16 November 1893-11 March 1894. Issued to all those participating in actions taken in Sierra Leone and Gambia.

"GAMBIA 1894"—23 February-13 March 1894. This bar was awarded for considerable fighting and casualties suffered during the short period of operations against Chief Fodi Silah.

"BENIN RIVER 1894"—August-November 1894. Recipients were members of a small, mainly naval force sent up the Benin River.

"BRASS RIVER 1895"—17-26 February 1895. Issued to those men taking part in the expedition against King Koko.

"1896-98"—27 November 1896-27 June 1898. Awarded to the men involved in several punitive expeditions into the Northern Territories of the Gold Coast. A seldom-seen clasp.

"NIGER 1897"—6 January-26 February 1897. Issued to those members of an expedition to the Western Provinces of Niger. This is a rare bar.

"BENIN 1897"—6 February-7 August 1897. This bar was awarded to members of a punitive expedition in the Benin Territory.

"DAWKITA 1897"—28 March 1897. Awarded to forty-two men of the Gold Coast Constabulary for the defense of Dawkita when under attack from Sofa tribesmen.

"1897-98"—September 1897-August 1898. Awarded to members of the Lagos Frontier Force for expeditions against the Ebos.

"1898"—Awarded to those who took part in any of the expeditions during 1898 noted for the previous bar.

"SIERRA LEONE 1898-99"—18 February 1898-9 March 1899. Awarded to the members of two expeditions involving a small naval brigade and native troops.

"1899"—February-May 1899. Issued to members of expeditions in Southern Nigeria.

"1900"—4 January-8 May 1900. This rare bar was awarded to members of the expedition to Kaduna and also for the Munshi expedition. ✕

British South Africa Company's Medal 1890–1897

In 1896, the British South Africa Company was sanctioned by the Queen to issue a medal to troops engaged in the Matabeleland Uprising of 1893, and, in 1897, another for those engaged in Rhodesia in 1896. In 1897, yet a third medal was sanctioned for those troops who operated in Mashonaland in 1897. All three of these medals are identical except for the name and date above the lion on the reverse. In 1927, a similar medal was authorized to recognize service in Mashonaland in 1890; there is neither a place named nor a date on the reverse. A "MASHONALAND 1890" clasp was also authorized with this medal.

The obverse bears the crowned and veiled head of Queen Victoria with the legend "VICTORIA REGINA." The reverse bears a charging lion with a spear in its chest, a mimosa bush in the background, and a native shield and spears in the foreground. Above are the name and date of the campaign for which the medal was originally made, while below is the legend "BRITISH SOUTH AFRICA COMPANY." The 1.40" wide ribbon of four yellow and three dark blue stripes is narrower than the suspender; and the suspender is wide and flat, with representations of roses, shamrocks and thistles. The suspender has a claw attachment sweated to the medal. Naming is usually done in engraved capitals, which sometimes will be found sloping. Those medals struck for Matabeleland and Rhodesia are also found with indented capitals.

A total of four bars were authorized for issue with this medal, as follows:

"MASHONALAND 1890"—1 June-12 September 1890. Due to incursions in the name of exploration and colonization made by the Portuguese, representations made to the Portuguese by the British were followed up by a field column into the contested territory. However, a confrontation did not actually occur, as the Portuguese retired from the field. Consequently, this medal was not awarded for combatant service. The medal roll contains six hundred and eighty-seven names, and a total of two hundred and seven medals were issued.

British South Africa Company's Medal, 1890-1897 (Obverse)

British South Africa Company's Medal (Reverse)

"MATABELELAND 1893"—16 October-24 December 1893. In July 1893, the Mashonas were attacked by the Matabele, followed by an attack on the British at Fort Victoria. Nominally under the control of King Lobengula, the Matabeles needed to be punished, and punished they were! It was during these expeditions that a force of thirty men were cut off by rising flood waters on the wrong side of the river, and were attacked by overwhelming numbers of Matabele warriors. The small force made an epic stand that remains a memorable one in military history. A total of 1,574 medals were awarded.

"RHODESIA 1896"—24 March-31 December 1896. In 1895, the territories subject to the British South Africa Company were named "Rhodesia," after Cecil Rhodes, with the country being split into Northern and Southern Rhodesia. In 1896, the Matabeles revolted, later being joined by the Mashonas; martial law was declared and expeditions formed to put down the rebellion. After many excursions and defeats of the natives, a meeting was held between Cecil Rhodes and the native chieftains at which peace was finally declared. Those who had been awarded the Matabeleland Medal, or who later were awarded the undated medal previously described, were presented a bar inscribed "RHODESIA 1896" to add to their medal.

"MASHONALAND 1897"—24 March-31 October 1897. The troubles supposedly settled by the peace talks of 1896 never really were resolved, and were instead re-ignited almost immediately. This called for a number of expeditionary forces to be sent to capture the kraals of the rebellious native chiefs. Final surrender was achieved on 29 October 1897. This medal is the rarest of those that bear a place name and date. ×

Central Africa Medal 1891–1898

This medal was first issued in 1895 to commemorate a variety of small campaigns and expeditions against unruly tribes in Central and East Africa between 1891 and 1894. The medal was reissued in 1899 for operations against tribes in Central Africa from 1894 to 1899. Ten separate expeditions were conducted from 1891-1894, most of them having been waged against tribes that were preying upon their neighbors,

or that opposed British rule over their country. No British regiment was entitled to this medal, although the award was given to a few officers and NCOs detached for duty with native troops.

This medal itself is identical to the one awarded for East and West Africa 1887-1900—displaying the same obverse and reverse. The only major difference is that the 1.25" ribbon, with three equal stripes of black, white, and brown, is sus-

pended from a small swiveling ring and claw mount attached to the top of the medal. In 1899, the medal was awarded with a straight suspension and a clasp for "CENTRAL AFRICA 1894-98." The majority of medals were awarded to Ugandan and Sudanese troops, while most of those without a clasp were issued to Indian troops. Some medals are found unnamed; some impressed; and still others engraved. ✕

Right—**Central Africa Medal, 1891-98** *(Obverse)*

Far Right—**Central Africa Medal** *(Reverse)*

Mark Razanauskas Collection

India General Service Medal 1895–1902

In view of the fact that the India General Service Medal of 1854 already had twenty-three clasps issued for it, the government decided it was time for a new medal, which was created in 1896. Issued in silver to British and Indian troops and in bronze to native auxiliaries, this award is generally referred to as the "India 1895 Medal." Queen Victoria died before the last bar for this medal was issued, so the final bar is found on the Edward VII issue of the medal, which has the "1895" date removed from the reverse.

Since the bar "Punjab Frontier 1897-98" wasn't awarded until June of 1898, one may question why the date was not removed at that time, since it appears almost incongruous for bars for operations in 1897-98 and 1901-02 to be awarded to a medal bearing an 1895 date. When the Edward VII version of the medal was produced, the British elected not to strike a new medal—somewhat strange since the obverse was new and the reverse was altered.

The obverse bears the crowned and veiled bust of Queen Victoria, adorned with earrings, necklace, and pendant, wearing the Ribbon and Star of the Garter, surrounded by the legend "VICTORIA REGINA ET IMPERATRIX." The reverse displays the figures of a British and Indian soldier, standing, with both supporting the Royal Standard. The British soldier holds the barrel of his rifle in his right hand, while the Indian soldier rests his left hand on his sword. The word "INDIA" is to the left, with "1895" on the right of the field. The 1.25" wide ribbon has three red stripes and two green stripes of equal width, suspended from a silver scroll bar with a claw attachment riveted to the medal. Names of the recipient are most often engraved; however, those medals with the two clasps "Punjab Frontier 1897-98" and "Malakand 1897" are generally found with indented capitals.

Far Left—**India General Service Medal, 1895-1902** *(Obverse)*

Left—**India General Service Medal, bars "Tirah 1897-98" and "Punjab Frontier 1897-98"**

The Gordon Highlanders at Dargai, 20 October 1897. Print: Allan Stewart

Storming of Dargai Heights, 20 October 1897, showing Piper Findlater, 1st Bn Gordon Highlanders, winning the V. C. Painting by Veneker Hamilton

35th Sikhs, fighting a rearguard action against tribesmen during the operations of the Malakand Field Force. Watercolor by E. J. Hobday

Top—**India General Service Medal, bar "Waziristan 1901-02" Edward VII** *(Obverse)*

Bottom—**India General Service Medal, bar "Waziristan 1901-02." Note the erased exergue.** *(Reverse)*

Top—**India General Service Medal, bars "Punjab Frontier 1897-98" and "Relief of Chitral 1896"** *(Reverse)*

Bottom—**India General Service Medal, bars "Tirah 1897-98," "Punjab Frontier 1897-98" and "Relief of Chitral"**

Seven bars were authorized for this medal, as follows:

"DEFENCE OF CHITRAL 1895"— 3 March-19 April 1895. Clasps awarded to those troops of the small garrison of Chitral who survived a seven week siege.

"RELIEF OF CHITRAL 1895"—7 March 1895-15 August 1895. Awarded to all members of the relief column that had fought through to relieve the siege.

"PUNJAB FRONTIER 1897-98"—10 June 1897-6 April 1898. Recipients were the troops involved in the defense of Shabkadr Fort, the Mohmand Field Force, and the Tirah Expeditionary Force.

"MALAKAND 1897"—26 July-2 August 1897. Awarded to the troops involved in the defense and relief of Chakdara and Malakand.

"SAMANA 1897"—22 August-2 October 1897. Earned by troops involved in the operations on Samana Ridge, the defense of Fort Gulistan, and especially for the heroic twenty-one Sikh defenders of the Saragai post who, for four days, held off the attacks of 10,000 Afridis before being overwhelmed and massacred to the last man.

"TIRAH 1897-98"—2 October 1897-6 April 1898. This clasp was awarded to men of the Tirah Expeditionary Force, including the Kurram and Peshawar Columns, and the Rawalpindi Brigade. Line of communication troops in the Swat Valley also received this clasp. Recipients were well-entitled to this clasp, for it commemorates over three hundred killed and a thousand wounded during the course of the campaign—one in which Afridi sniping played a large part.

"WAZIRISTAN 1901-02"—23 November 1901-10 March 1902. This is the clasp awarded to the second issue (King Edward VII) medal for all troops involved in a four month campaign of fighting, raids, and road building against the Mahsuds. ✕

Ashanti Star
7 December 1895 – 17 January 1896

The Ashanti Expedition was born of British concern over the native tribes' propensity for—among other dreadful acts—human flesh, human sacrifice, and the love of torture. The expedition, led by Major General Sir F. C. Scott, was comprised of approximately 2,000 Imperial and Colonial troops, and operated successfully against King Prempeh, defeating his warriors and destroying his capital of Coomassie.

The distinctive gunmetal Star is four-pointed, with Saint Andrew's Cross visible between the points. The Imperial Crown is at center, surrounded by a band which bears the inscription "ASHANTI 1896." On the reverse face is the legend "FROM THE QUEEN" in raised letters. The name and regiment of the recipient are engraved on the arms of the cross. The 1.25" ribbon is yellow, with two black stripes near the edge. It is suspended from the medal by a ring. There were no clasps awarded for this medal. ✕

Right—**Ashanti Star, 1896** *(Obverse)*

Far Right—**Ashanti Star** *(Reverse)*

Queen's Sudan Medal 1896–1897

Awarded in both silver and bronze, The Queen's Sudan Medal was issued to all who took part in any of the first six actions in the re-conquest of the Sudan for which the Khedive's Medal—which followed immediately—was awarded. It will be remembered that the Egyptians had suffered the loss of the Sudan Province to the Mahdi and his followers. The possibilities of anarchy and a power vacuum in the lost province, especially during this period of European colonization, were not to be taken lightly.

It was the Italians' defeat by the Abyssinians at Adowa in 1896 that catalyzed thoughts of an eventual recovery of the Sudan (and revenge for Gordon), and ultimately led the British to take action, commencing with the advance of Kitchener and his Anglo-Egyptian army up the Nile. Since no clasps were issued

Portrait of a young corporal prior to going overseas to Egypt.

Wupperfeld collection

Queen's Sudan Medal, 1896-97
(Obverse)

Queen's Sudan Medal, 1896-97
(Reverse)

for this medal, actions for which clasps were added to the Khedive's Medal will relate the story of the battles fought.

The obverse bears the crowned half-figure of Queen Victoria, surrounded by the legend "VICTORIA REGINA ET IMPERATRIX." The reverse face bears the finely balanced figure of Victory, seated, holding a palm branch in her right hand and a laurel wreath in her left. At her feet, on a plaque supported by three lilies, is the word "SUDAN." Behind, and on either side, are the British and Egyptian flags. Altogether, this depicts one of the most appealing figures of

Victory. The 1.25" wide ribbon has yellow on the left half, while the right half is black; a thin red line divides the two colors. It is said that these colors were chosen to represent the yellow desert and the black dervishes, divided by the thin red line of British troops. The ribbon is suspended from the medal by a plain straight suspender with a claw mount riveted to the medal. Naming varies considerably: Some are engraved in neat, sloping capitals, and some in upright capitals; a few have been impressed in thin Roman capitals, others in Arabic; still others are without any name. ✕

Khedive's Sudan Medal 1896-1908

Sanctioned by a special order of the Egyptian Army on 12 February 1897, this medal was issued to commemorate the re-conquest of Dongala Province. Made in both silver and bronze, it was to be worn to the right of the Khedive's Bronze Star. The medal is rarely seen awarded to British troops with more than two bars (for "Atbara" and "Khartoum"). It may be seen awarded without clasps to troops who served in the northern or eastern Sudan in 1896. The first two clasps were issued to those who took part in battles during the 1896 retaking of Dongala.

With the further advances made in 1897 an additional two clasps were awarded; while in 1898 the advance on—followed by the battle for—Khartoum saw the defeat of the Dervishes at both Atbara and Khartoum (Omdurman). This was the campaign in which British troops played a major part, after which pacification of the balance of the Sudan was left to Egyptian and Sudanese troops.

The obverse of the medal bears an Arabic inscription that translates "ABBAS HILMI THE SECOND" with the Mohammedan year 1314, which by the Christian calendar is 1897. The reverse is quite ornate, with an oval shield bearing three stars and crescents in the center, and surrounded by flags and lances. The whole is superimposed upon two crossed rifles and two cannons, with a mound of cannon balls in the center. Below is a plaque inscribed "THE RECONQUEST OF THE SUDAN, 1314" in Arabic. The 1.50" wide ribbon is yellow (the desert) with a broad blue stripe (the Nile) running down the mid-

Khedive's Sudan Medal, 1896-1908 (Obverse)

Khedive's Sudan Medal (Reverse)

dle. The medal is suspended by a plain, straight suspender and claw mount which is sweated to the medal. Naming to British troops was in sloping capitals, while medals named to Indian troops are usually done in script. Medals to native troops are generally unnamed—the few that are named being inscribed in Arabic.

Fifteen clasps, named in both English and Arabic, were autho-

rized for issue with the medal, as follows:

"FIRKET"—7 June 1896.
Awarded to those present at the defeat of the Emir Osman Azraq at Firket.

"HAFIR"—19-26 September 1896.
Presented to those troops present at the battle of Hafir on the west bank of the Nile opposite Kerma.

The Battle of The Atbara, showing Privates Watt, Smith, and MacDonald of the Cameron Highlanders. Wupperfeld collection

The "stand-to" at the Battle of Omdurman. Wupperfeld collection

"ABU HAMED"—7 July 1897. Awarded to members of Major-General A. Hunter's force that captured Abu Hamed.

"SUDAN 1897"—15 July-6 November 1897. Not awarded for any particular action, but given to those already in receipt of the medal who were south of both Kerma and No. 6 Station between the dates indicated.

"THE ATBARA"—8 April 1898. Rarely found singly, this clasp was presented to all those at the battle of the Atbara, fought against the Dervish Army under the command of Emir Mahmoud.

"KHARTOUM"—2 September 1898. Though entry into Khartoum occurred immediately after, this clasp was actually for the Battle of Omdurman. It is unusual for a clasp to be inscribed other than for the battle fought.

"GEDAREF"—7 September-26 December 1898. Earned by all those who took part in the fighting in the Eastern Sudan against Ahmed Fedil, who escaped after the fall of Gedaref.

"GEDID"—22 November 1899. After managing to escape from Gedaref, Ahmed Fedil rejoined the Khalifa, who had been driven from the battlefield at Omdurman. With their men, they attacked the British gunboat "Sultan," resulting in a force of 2,300 men being sent to pursue them. On 22 November, the forces joined battle at Gedid, with the Khalifa and Ahmed Fedil being killed and their troops defeated. Thus ended the re-conquest of the Sudan.

"SUDAN 1899"—Presented to all troops who served on either the Blue or the White Nile south of Khartoum during 1899.

"BAHR-EL-GHAZAL 1900-02"—13 December 1900-28 April 1902. Awarded for policing operations in the Bahr-El-Ghazal Province.

"JEROK"—January-March 1904. Awarded to participants in the attack on slave raider Ibrahim Wad Mahmud on the Blue Nile near the Abyssinian border.

"NYAM-NYAM"—January-May 1905. Awarded to all those involved in the restoration of order in the Bahr-El Ghazal Province near the border with the Belgian Congo.

"TALODI"—2-15 June 1905. Presented to troops involved with quelling the uprising of the Abu Rufas which occurred in the Nubas Mountains at Eliri.

"KATFIA"—April 1908. Awarded for the suppression of the uprising of Mohammed Wad Habuba, a murdering self-styled prophet who was captured and hanged.

"NYIMA"—1-21 November 1908. Issued for a punitive expedition into the Nyima Hills. ⨯

East and Central Africa Medal 1897–1899

According to Army Order dated 29 February 1899, Her Majesty was "graciously pleased to approve" a medal called the "EAST AND CENTRAL AFRICA MEDAL 1897-98," being granted to those forces employed in military operations in the Uganda Protectorate during 1897-98.

The obverse of the medal bears the half-length effigy of Queen Victoria wearing earrings, necklace and pendant; crowned and veiled, with a small Imperial Crown placed above the lace veil; wearing the Star of the Garter, the Royal Order of Victoria and Albert, and the Imperial Order of the Crown of India; while holding a scepter in her right hand. Around the figure is the legend "VICTORIA REGINA ET IMPERATRIX."

The reverse bears a figure of Britannia standing in front of a British lion, facing right, with her outstretched left hand offering a palm branch and scroll toward the rising sun. Her right hand holds a trident. In the exergue are the words "EAST AND CENTRAL AFRICA" in capital letters. The 1.25" half-red and half-yellow ribbon is suspended from a straight bar which is attached to the medal by means of an ornamental clip fastened to the medal by a rivet.

Four clasps were issued for various expeditions, as follows:

"LUBWA'S"—23 September 1897-24 February 1898. Granted to all those forces taking part in operations in Uganda against the Sudanese mutineers who were holding Fort Lubwa.

East and Central Africa Medal, 1897-1899 *(Obverse)*

East and Central Africa Medal *(Reverse)*

"UGANDA 1897-98"—20 July 1897-19 March 1898. Awarded to all those who took part in operations in Uganda other than those actions conducted against the Sudanese mutineers.

"1898"—April-August 1898. Awarded to all forces employed against the Ogaden Somalis during this period.

"UGANDA 1899"—21 March-2 May 1899. Granted to all Imperial and Colonial troops employed in the operations against Kabarega in the Uganda Protectorate.

All clasps have a thin straight line paralleling the inside of the plain raised border. Naming is by indented capitals as well as by thin engraved capitals. ✕

British North Borneo Company's Medals 1897–1937

While military in nature, and sanctioned for wear by members of the military who had been awarded the medal, these medals were also issued to Company members who were involved in small punitive expeditions against troublesome native tribes over a forty year period. Two distinctly different medals were awarded, with three different ribbons. These medals were issued in both silver and bronze.

The first medal was issued for a campaign against Mat Selah in 1897, with twelve silver and seventy-four bronze unnamed medals awarded. In 1898 a further expedition was conducted against Mat Selah, with another five silver and forty-seven bronze named-and-numbered medals awarded. In 1899-1900, a last campaign against Mat Selah was mounted, resulting in Mat Selah being killed and a new (second award) medal being issued to the victors.

The obverse of the first medal bears the North Borneo Company shield, flanked by two natives. The native on the left is holding a shield, while the one on the right holds a long sword with his left hand. Above, a pair of arms hold the Company's flag; below is a flowing banner bearing a Latin inscription, and backed by floral decorations. The reverse depicts the British lion backed by the flag of the North Borneo Company against a background of native bushes, with "BRITISH NORTH BORNEO" above, and a laurel wreath below. The 1.25" ribbon was originally watered gold overall, but in 1917 this was changed to include maroon edges. Still

British North Borneo Company's Medal, 1897-1937, First Award *(Obverse)*

British North Borneo Company's Medal, First Award *(Reverse)*

later, a dark blue stripe was added to the center. Suspension is by an ornate suspender similar to that seen on the India General Service Medal, with claw mount sweated to the medal. One "PUNITIVE EXPEDITION" clasp was authorized for this first award.

The second medal's obverse bears the Company's shield, with "NORTH BORNEO COMPANY"

above and, below, the date "1900." The reverse of the second medal shows two arms supporting the Company flag within a wreath, while around the wreath is the Latin inscription "PERGO ET PERAGO." The 1.25" ribbon is yellow with a central green stripe and is suspended from the medal by a straight suspender and claw mount riveted to the medal. One bar for the 1900 "TAMBUNAN" campaign was authorized for this medal. The clasp is quite attractive, featuring indented edges, rosettes on the bottom of each end, and scrollwork outlining the inside of the clasp.

In 1915, a small relief expedition was dispatched to the village of Rundum to suppress an attack mounted by rebellious natives. A medal was struck for award to members of the expedition, but it was done only in silver, with a total of one hundred and thirteen awarded. This medal is identical to the one of 1897, but bears the clasp "RUNDUM." The final medal issued in this series was sanctioned in April, 1937 and is known as the General Service Medal. Awarded only in silver, only forty-two awards have been traced. The obverse of the medal is identical to the 1897 issue. The reverse depicts Britannia seated, holding the trident and shield, together with an inscription. The half-yellow, half-green ribbon is suspended from the medal by a ring and claw mount. No clasp was authorized for this medal. ×

British North Borneo Company's Medal, 1897-1937, Second Award (Obverse)

British North Borneo Company's Medal, Second Award (Reverse)

Queen's South Africa Medal
11 October 1899 – 31 May 1902

This medal is the most common in the Victorian series of medals, awarded for services during the Boer War of 1899-1902. The Boer War, or the South African War, was not the usual little conflict that the British were used to fighting with armies composed mostly of native troops. This was a serious, major war, with many characteristics of the later World Wars. Large armies were involved, with great numbers of poorly-trained volunteers; huge technological changes were occurring; and unforetold logistical problems developed on a scale never before experienced.

The Boer War was precipitated by British insistence on suzerainty over the Transvaal, with the Dutch settlers resisting and insisting on their rights as a sovereign nation. The British were given an ultimatum to relinquish claim on the Transvaal or suffer the consequences. Throughout the winter months of 1899 (June through September constitute the winter season in South Africa), both sides prepared for the oncoming war and waited. When the terms of the ultimatum expired on 11 October 1899, Boer Commandos crossed the border of the Transvaal; invaded the Cape Colony and Natal; and war was commenced.

It was a war that can be divided into three phases: Phase One, wherein the Boers invade the British Colonies; Phase Two, where the British invade the Boer territories; and Phase Three, in which the Boers refuse to accept outward defeat and continue a protracted, bitter twenty-month guerrilla campaign against British suppressive tactics. This was a war that required brains and skill

on the part of the British generals—a commodity in extremely short supply at the beginning of the war. The war ended only after the British resorted to the use of concentration camps for women and children—and even economic warfare, which included the burning of farms and cropland.

This award is complex due to the literally hundreds of different units serving during the war and the twenty-six clasps that were authorized. There were approximately 178,000 medals issued, with the majority issued in silver, and a very few issued in bronze to Indian transport personnel. The

Sounding the Call! Wupperfeld collection

Top—**Queen's South Africa Medal, 1899-1902, Silver** *(Obverse)*

Bottom—**Queen's South Africa Medal, Silver** *(Reverse)*

Top—**Queen's South Africa Medal, 1899-1902, Bronze** *(Obverse)*

Bottom—**Queen's South Africa Medal, Bronze** *(Reverse)*

maximum number of bars to any one medal is nine for the Army and eight for the Navy. There are two different strikings for this medal. The first may be readily identified because the wreath of Britannia points towards the "R" in Africa, while in the second strike it points to the "F." The first issue also bears the dates "1899-1900" on the reverse in raised figures, a mistake that was quickly corrected. Lord Strathcona's Horse (Canada) was the only unit to receive a limited number of the medals as they were first struck. Approximately 3,750 of the medals with erased dates were subsequently issued to Canadian units.

The obverse of the medal bears the bust of Queen Victoria, veiled and crowned, wearing the Order of the Garter, adorned with earrings, necklace and pendant, and the Royal Order of Victoria and Albert, with the legend "VICTORIA REGINA ET IMPERATRIX." The reverse bears the helmeted figure of Britannia standing, in her left hand holding a standard, and in her right a laurel wreath extended. Behind Britannia's figure, troops are marching from a hilly setting onward to the coast, with a man-of-war seen in the left background. The legend "SOUTH AFRICA" appears above, and in the exergue "G.W.DE SAVLLES." The 1.25" wide ribbon has a broad central orange stripe between two narrow stripes of dark blue with red borders. The ribbon is suspended from a straight suspender with an ornamental claw mount riveted to the medal. Naming is either impressed or engraved in various styles around the rim, and the owner's unit is included. The clasps authorized for issuance with this medal are as follows:

"CAPE COLONY"—11 October 1899-31 May 1902. Issued to all troops in the Cape Colony during the prescribed period who received no clasp for any action already specified for the Cape Colony, nor the "NATAL" clasp.

A scene at the Battle of Elandslaagte, 21 October 1899. *Illustrated London News*

"NATAL"—11 October 1899-17 May 1900. Granted to all troops who served in Natal between 11 October 1899 and 11 June 1900 (inclusive) who were not eligible for an action in Natal nor the Cape Colony clasp as specified.

"RHODESIA"—11 October 1899-17 May 1900. Authorized for all troops under the command of Lt. General Sir F. Carrington and Col. Plummer in Rhodesia during the above dates who received no clasp for the relief of Mafeking.

"RELIEF OF MAFEKING"—17 May 1900. Awarded to all men under the command of Col. Mahon, and all troops under the command of Col. Plummer, between 11 October 1899 and 17 May 1900 (inclusive) who were south of an east-west line drawn through Palachwe.

"DEFENCE OF KIMBERLEY"— 15 October 1899-15 February 1900. Issued to all troops in the garrison of Kimberley between the dates shown.

"TALANA"—30 October 1899. Awarded to all troops present under the command of Lt. General Sir W. Penn Symon on 20 October who were north of an east-west line drawn through Waschbank Station.

"ELANDSLAAGTE"—21 October 1899. Granted to all troops at Elandslaagte on 21 October 1899 who were on the right bank of the Sunday river and north of an east-west line through Buy's farm.

"DEFENCE OF LADYSMITH"—3 November 1899-28 February 1900. Authorized for all troops in the Ladysmith defense force between the dates shown.

"BELMONT"—23 November 1899. Issued to all troops under the command of Lt. General Lord Methuen who were north of Witteputs (exclusive) on 23 November 1899.

"MODDER RIVER"—28 November 1899. Awarded to all the troops under the command of Lt. General Lord Methuen who were north of Honey Nest Kloof (exclusive) and south of the Magersfontein ridge (exclusive) on 28 November 1899.

"TUGELA HEIGHTS"—14-27 February 1900. Issued to all troops of the Natal Field Force, exclusive of the Ladysmith garrison, employed in the operations north of an east-west line extending through Chieveley Station between 14 and 27 February 1900.

Pipe Corporal McKay rallying the Argylls at Magersfontein. *Illustrated London News*

British dead in the shallow trenches of Spion Kop, 1900.

Charge of the 9th and 16th Lancers at Klip Drift, 15 February 1900.
By W. S. Small

"RELIEF OF KIMBERLEY"—15 February 1900. Granted to all troops in the relief column under Lt. General French who marched from Klip Drift on 15 February 1900; and to all of the 6th Division under Lt. General Kelly-Kenny who were within 7,000 yards of Klip Drift on 15 February 1900.

"PAARDEBERG"—17-26 February 1900. Issued to all troops who were within 7,000 yards of General Cronje's final lager between midnight of 17 February and midnight of 26 February 1900; and also to all troops within 7,000 yards of Koodoe's Rand Drift between those same dates.

"ORANGE FREE STATE"—28 February 1900-31 May 1902. Granted to all troops in the Orange River Colony at any time between the preceding dates who received no clasp that has been specified for an action in the Orange River Colony.

"RELIEF OF LADYSMITH"—15 December 1899-28 February 1900. Awarded to all troops in Natal north of, and including, Estcourt between 15 December 1899 and 28 February 1900 (both dates inclusive).

"DRIEFONTEIN"—10 March 1900. Issued to all troops at Army Headquarters, as well as to those who were part of Lt. General French's column which advanced from Poplar Grove on 10 March 1900.

"WEPENER"—9-25 April 1900. Granted to the troops engaged in the defense of Wepener between the dates indicated.

"DEFENCE OF MAFEKING"—13 October 1899-17 May 1900. Awarded to all troops in the garrison of Mafeking between 13 October 1899 and 17 May 1900. Approximately 1,150 of these clasps were awarded.

The attack of the 58th at Laing's Nek, 12 June 1900. After a painting by Lady Butler

"TRANSVAAL"—24 May 1900-31 May 1902. Awarded to all troops in the Transvaal at any time between 24 May 1900 and 31 May 1902 who received no clasp for an action in the Transvaal that has already been specified.

"JOHANNESBURG"—31 May 1900. Issued to all troops who, on 29 May 1900, were north of an east-west line through Klip River Station (exclusive) and east of a north-south line through Krugersdorp Station (inclusive).

"LAING'S NEK"—12 June 1900. Granted to all members of the Natal Field Force employed in the operations, and north of an east-west line through Newcastle between 2-9 June, 1900 (both dates inclusive).

"DIAMOND HILL"—11-12 June 1900. Presented to all troops who, on the dates specified, were east of a north-south line through Silverton Siding and north of an east-west line through Vlakfontein.

"WITTEBERGEN"—Issued to all troops within the boundaries of a line from Harrismith to Bethlehem, thence to Senekal and Clocolan, along the Basuto border, and back to Harrismith, between 1-29 July 1900 (both dates inclusive).

The last charge on Pieter's Hill by the 2nd Royal Irish Fusiliers. Note the "ZAR" marked wooden box in the right foreground. R. Caton Woodville

"BELFAST"—26-27 August 1900. Presented to all troops who, on 26 or 27 August 1900, were east of a north-south line through Wonderfontein (garrison not eligible), and west of a north-south line through Carolina.

"SOUTH AFRICA 1901"—This clasp was awarded to those who were not eligible for the King's Medal even though they had served at the front between 1 January and 31 December 1901.

"SOUTH AFRICA 1902"—This clasp was awarded to those who were not eligible for the King's Medal even though they had served at the front between 1 January and 31 May 1902. ×

Right—**Queen's South Africa Medal, bar "Elandslaagte"**

Far Right—**Queen's South Africa Medal, bar "Defence Of Kimberley"**

Studio portrait before going overseas, Boer War. Wupperfeld collection

Queen's South Africa Medal, bar "Defence of Mafeking"

Queen's South Africa Medal, bar "Modder River"

Before Going Overseas, Gordon Highlander, c. 1900. Wupperfeld collection

Queen's South Africa Medal, bar "Defence of Ladysmith"

Queen's South Africa Medal, bars "Defence of Mafeking" and "Rhodesia"

Queen's South Africa Medal, bars "South Africa 1902" and "Cape Colony" *(Obverse)*

Queen's South Africa Medal *(Reverse)*, showing clasp mounting.

Queen's South Africa Medal, bars "Transvaal" and "Natal"

Queen's South Africa Medal, bars "Belfast," "Orange Free State," and "Cape Colony"

Queen's South Africa Medal, bars "Transvaal", "Orange Free State," and "Natal"

Queen's South Africa Medal, bars "South Africa 1901," "Wittebergen," and "Cape Colony"

Queen's New Years Eve's gift to soldiers in the Boer War. It was filled with either candy, cigarettes, or pipe tobacco. Author's collection

Queen's South Africa Medal, bars "Transvaal," "Orange Free State," and "Relief of Kimberley"

Queen's South Africa Medal, bars "Wittebergen," "Transvaal," "Wepener," and "Cape Colony"

Queen's South Africa Medal, bars "Wittebergen," "Driefontein," "Paardeberg," and "Cape Colony"

Queen's South Africa Medal, bars "South Africa 1901," "Orange Free State," "Rhodesia," and "Cape Colony" *(Note clasps positioned to reverse)*

Queen's South Africa Medal, bars "Belfast," "Laing's Nek," "Defence of Ladysmith," and "Elandslaagte"

Queen's South Africa Medal, bars "South Africa 1901," "Transvaal," "Relief of Ladysmith," and "Cape Colony"

Tea Canister in the shape of a Boer War Artillery Shell...Note the fuse at the top. Wupperfeld collection

Queen's South Africa Medal, bars "South Africa 1901," "Transvaal," "Rhodesia," and "Cape Colony"

Queen's South Africa Medal, bars "Orange Free State," "Cape Colony," "Transvaal," "Defence of Ladysmith," and "Talana"

New Year's Day, 1900 Gift Box from the Scots to Scottish Soldiers in the Boer War. Wupperfeld collection

Queen's South Africa Medal, bars "South Africa 1901," "Wittebergen," "Diamond Hill," "Johannesburg," and "Cape Colony"

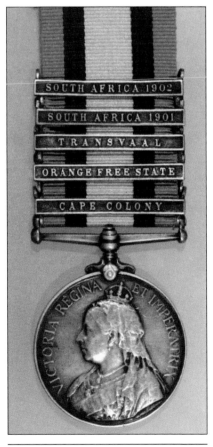

Queen's South Africa Medal, bars "South Africa 1902," "South Africa 1901," "Transvaal," "Orange Free State," and "Cape Colony"

Queen's South Africa Medal, bars "Transvaal," "Relief of Ladysmith," "Orange Free State," "Tugela Heights," and "Cape Colony"

Queen's South Africa Medal, bars "Laing's Nek," "Transvaal," "Relief of Ladysmith," "Orange Free State," and "Tugela Heights"

Queen's South Africa Medal, bars "Orange Free State," "Cape Colony," "Transvaal," "Defence of Ladysmith," and "Talana"

Queen's South Africa Medal, bars "Cape Colony," "Belfast," "Laing's Nek," "Relief of Ladysmith," "Orange Free State," and "Tugela Heights"

Queen's South Africa Medal, bars "South Africa 1901," "Belfast," "Johannesburg," "Driefontein," "Paardeberg," and "Cape Colony"

Queen's South Africa Medal, bars "Belfast," "Diamond Hill," "Johannesburg," "Driefontein," "Paardeberg," and "Relief of Kimberley"

Queen's South Africa Medal, bars "South Africa 1901," "Belfast," "Diamond Hill," "Johannesburg," "Driefontein," "Modder River," and "Belmont"

King's South Africa Medal 1899-1902

Queen Victoria died during the Boer War. King Edward VII then authorized a second war medal, bearing his effigy, to recognize the services rendered by British troops during the latter phases of the campaign in South Africa, and to reward those individuals who, by virtue of their long and dedicated service in the field, had brought the war to a successful conclusion. This second medal is called the "KING'S SOUTH AFRICA MEDAL."

This medal, in silver only, was granted to all troops in the British, Imperial, and Colonial Forces; to civilian Medical Practitioners and others employed in military hospitals in South Africa; as well as to all Nursing Sisters, provided that they were serving in South Africa on or after 1 January 1902, and on that date had completed eighteen months war service or completed such service prior to 1 June 1902.

The obverse of the medal bears the bust of King Edward VII in Field Marshall's uniform, with top coat, wearing the Star and Ribbon of the Order of the Garter, the badge of the G.C.B., and other decorations and medals. The legend "EDWARDVS VII RES IMPERATOR" appears on the circumference surrounding the bust. The reverse of this medal is identical to the Queen's South Africa Medal. The 1.25" wide ribbon has three stripes of equal width in orange, white, and green, worn so the green stripe is on the right. The ribbon is suspended from the medal by a straight bar with ornamental clip riveted to the medal.

Naming is done either in small impressed capitals or in engraved upper and lower case letters.

Two clasps were authorized, inscribed "SOUTH AFRICA 1901" to all who served in South Africa between 1 January 1901 and 31 December 1901 (both dates inclusive); and "SOUTH AFRICA 1902" to all who served in South Africa between 1 January 1902 and 31 May 1902, both dates inclusive. ✕

King's South Africa Medal, bars "South Africa 1901" and "South Africa 1902" *(Obverse)*

King's South Africa Medal, 1899-1902 *(Reverse)*

Queen's Mediterranean Medal 1899–1902

Authorized in 1902 by King Edward VII, this medal, which is identical to the Queen's South Africa Medal save for one difference, was issued to all officers and men of the Militia who had volunteered for service abroad during the South African War. Numerous garrisons in the Mediterranean were withdrawn for service in South Africa, and these garrisons were replaced by the volunteer Militia battalions. Troops stationed on St. Helena, an important P.O.W. base, were also declared eligible for this medal. Approximately 5,000 of the medals were issued.

Both the obverse and reverse faces of the Mediterranean Medal are identical to the Queen's South Africa Medal, except that the words "SOUTH AFRICA" are replaced by the word "MEDITER-RANEAN." The ribbon and the suspension are also identical, with the naming either impressed or engraved in various styles. No clasp was authorized for wear with this medal. ✕

Right—**Queen's Mediterranean Medal** *(Obverse)*

Far Right—**Queen's Mediterranean Medal** *(Reverse)*

Defence of Kimberley Star 1899–1900

As this medal was not to be worn in uniform, it cannot be considered a campaign medal, but it is included here as an intrinsic part of the history of the South African War. In the first phase of that war, Boer Commandos bottled-up British forces in Ladysmith, Kimberley, and Mafeking. Strategically, the relief of Kimberley was not a priority of British "things to do." However, it was politically necessary since Cecil Rhodes, the most important figure in South Africa, was also under siege in Kimberley, demanding that the town immediately be relieved!

A force of 8,000 men under incompetent Lord Methuen was dispatched to deal with this unruly crowd of "farmers." On the way, they suffered through a battle at Belmont, entrenched Boers at Graspaan, the horrendous Battle of the Modder River, and the "butcher shop" of Magersfontein. Then, under command of Lord Roberts, the force turned the flank of the Boers and relieved the town in mid-February 1900.

The silver Star measures 1.875" by 1.625" and has six points, each of which has a small ball on the end. The obverse bears the Town Shield and the name "KIMBER-LEY" above, with the dates "1899-1900" below. Suspension is by means of an ornate foliate bar sewn to the ribbon, with a hook for the ring attached to the medal by means of an eye. At the top of the ribbon, a silver clasp bears the name of the recipient; the back of the clasp bearing a safety-pin-type attachment for wear. The 1" wide ribbon has equal red, white and blue stripes down the middle, with one yellow and one black edge. The reverse of the medal is marked in relief, "MAYOR'S SIEGE MEDAL, 1900." Records show that approximately 5,000 of these Stars were made and presented. ×

Defence of Kimberley Star, 1899-1900 *(Obverse)*

Defence of Kimberley Star *(Reverse)*

Transport Medal 1899-1902

This is not truly a campaign medal, but because of the unusual logistical problems caused by the war in South Africa, it is included here as a bit of wartime curiosa. This medal was sanctioned on 8 November 1903 for award to the Masters; 1st, 2nd and 3rd Officers; 1st, 2nd and 3rd Engineers; and the Pursers and Surgeons of merchant vessels used in the Transport Service assigned to take troops to South Africa and to China for service in the Boxer Rebellion. Eleven hospital ships along with one hundred and seventeen transports were employed during the two campaigns.

A total of 1,781 medals were issued. The obverse bears the bust of King Edward VII in Naval uniform with the legend "EDWARD VII REX ET IMPERATOR." The reverse bears a depiction of H.M.T. OPHIR, above which is a part of the map of the world and the Latin inscription "OB PATRIAM MILITIBUS PER MARE TRANSVECTIS ADJUTAM" (For services rendered in transporting troops by sea). The 1.25" wide ribbon is red with two dark blue stripes near the edge. Suspension is by means of a plain, straight, swiveling suspender with claw mount riveted to the medal. Two clasps were authorized for this medal: "SOUTH AFRICA 1899-1902" and "CHINA 1900." Those medals with the "CHINA 1900" clasp are considered quite rare.

An interesting side note to this medal is the fact that it was also to be issued to Merchant Marine officers in future wars who serve in transport duty. ✕

Far Left—**Transport Medal, 1899-1902** *(Obverse)*

Left—**Transport Medal** *(Reverse)*

Ashanti Medal
31 March – 25 December 1900

At the time that the Boer War was raging on, new troubles arose in both China and in Western Africa. British authorities in West Africa decided to seize the "Golden Stool"—the symbol of authority among the Ashanti tribes. Unsuccessful in their attempt, a rebellion of the natives soon followed.

British authorities, including the governor himself, were besieged in Kumassi with a small garrison of troops, and things were looking decidedly quite ugly. Three small columns were able to fight through and join the garrison, but it was not until two large columns of troops were dispatched that the city of Kumassi was recaptured, the siege raised, and the Ashanti beaten into submission once more.

A medal in silver and bronze (for native transport personnel and followers) was authorized to commemorate the campaign and was granted to all Imperial and Colonial troops attached to the Ashanti Field Force between 31 March and 25 December 1900 (both dates inclusive); also to all troops engaged in the defense of Kumassi; those involved in the relief column that left from Bekwai on 13 July and reached Kumassi on 15 July 1900; and to all in the relief column from Bekwai leaving on 4 August and arriving in Kumassi 5 August 1900.

The obverse of the medal bears the bust of King Edward VII in Field Marshal's uniform, with top coat, wearing the Star and Ribbon of the Order of the Garter, the badge of the G.C.B., and other decorations and medals. The surrounding legend is: "EDWARDVS VII REX IMPERATOR."

The reverse bears the British lion standing on a rise of ground

Ashanti Medal, 1900 *(Obverse)*

Ashanti Medal *(Reverse)*

overlooking a river with the rising sun on the left. Below, two spears—one is broken—rest upon a native shield, while on the right is a palm branch. On a scroll in the exergue is the word "ASHANTI." The medal is suspended from its 1.25" wide ribbon—which is green, with black edges and a black stripe down the middle—by a plain, straight bar with claw mount riveted to the medal. Names of recipients are

indented as well as engraved around the medal.

This was the first medal issued with King Edward VII's head on the obverse, which is similar to the King's South Africa Medal, but with the head in higher relief and much more distinct.

One clasp, "KUMASSI," was authorized for this medal. This medal is considered by collectors to be quite scarce and desirable. ✕

Third China War Medal
10 June – 31 December 1900

During the late 1890s, anti-foreign sentiment was on a rapid rise in China, based on hatred of foreign missionaries and their Christian Chinese converts, as well as hatred of foreign merchants who had carved China into separate spheres of influence and who dominated its trade by wielding overwhelming economic power. The name adopted by these nationalistic groups was "Fists of Righteous Harmony" or "Boxers," as they were popularly called.

Over a few explosive months in 1900, these fanatical sects, tacitly backed by the Manchu government, slaughtered hundreds of Christian missionaries and thousands of Chinese Christians, in addition to besieging the foreign settlement of Tientsin and the diplomatic community of Peking. Engaged in holding off the hordes of Boxers, as well as thousands of Imperial Chinese Army troops, the Peking legations were nearly devoid of supplies and ammunition by the time a multi-national force arrived to relieve them.

With a bumbling that verged on the tragi-comic, the soldiers and sailors of seven nations relieved the siege of Tientsin and then proceeded to fumble their way to Peking—arguing all the way as to who was in charge—while managing at times to march into their own lines of fire! When the international force finally stormed the walls of Peking, there ensued a violent orgy of looting, pillaging, and rape seldom seen on such an international scale. This was followed by more months of bloody revenge which included beheadings, hangings, and other such acts against the Boxer captives.

Third China War, 1900 *(Obverse)*

Third China War *(Reverse)*

To recognize all of these activities, in April 1902 King Edward VII confirmed the order given by Her late Majesty Queen Victoria that a medal be struck to commemorate these operations. Similar in pattern to medals granted for the earlier Chinese Wars, it was issued in silver and bronze.

The obverse of the medal bears the bust of Queen Victoria, crowned and veiled; adorned with earrings, necklace and pendant; wearing the Order of the Garter, and the Royal Order of Victoria and Albert; and surrounded by the legend "VICTORIA REGINA ET IMPERATRIX." The reverse displays a shield and the Royal Arms superimposed on a trophy of naval and military weapons, with a palm

Allies marching on Peking, with Indian cavalry to the fore. Third China War. Wupperfeld collection

tree behind. Above is the legend "ARMIS EXPOSCERE PACEM;" in the exergue, "CHINA 1900." The 1.25" wide yellow ribbon has red edges. Suspension is by means of a straight, plain bar with a claw mount riveted to the medal. The name of the recipient is in indented, thin, block capital letters for European troops and in engraved running script for Indian troops; while bronze medals issued to the locally hired transport workers were not named. ✕

Three clasps were authorized for the Third China War Medal—a maximum of two to any one recipient:

"DEFENCE OF LEGATIONS"—Approximately eighty-two clasps awarded to British troops forming a part of the legation guard. Medals with this clasp are most sought after by collectors.

"RELIEF OF PEKING"—Awarded to all officers and men involved in the relief column that stormed Peking.

"TAKU FORTS"—Issued almost exclusively to the Royal Navy, with the exception of one battalion of the 2nd Royal Welsh Fusiliers. This clasp is also very rare, as only six hundred and twenty were authorized. Naming for Royal Navy recipients is done in large impressed capitals.

Africa General Service Medal 1902–1956

47

This medal, in silver and bronze, was sanctioned in 1902 and had the desirable effect of standardizing awards for the various expeditions that were deployed in east and west Africa. There were three obverse types: that of King Edward VII (1902-1910); George V (1910-1920); and Queen Elizabeth II (1952-1956). Operations were almost continuous from 1902 through 1920, while there was a long hiatus between the second and third—the final medal being issued for operations against the Mau-Mau in Kenya.

Medals were mainly awarded to native troops, with some British officers and NCOs on detachment to native units also winning this award. The only time that the medal was awarded to a large British force was during the turmoil in Somalia from 1902-1904. The clasp "JIDBALLI" will always be found with the clasp "SOMALILAND 1902-1904." As will be seen by the naming of the clasps, operations in West Africa were centered mainly in Nigeria, while operations in East Africa were concentrated largely in the interior highlands, far from the coast. Four clasps were authorized for expeditions against the "Mad Mullah."

The obverse of the first issue of the medal bears the bust of King Edward VII (1902-1910) in Field Marshal's uniform, with top coat, wearing the Star and Ribbon of the Order of the Garter, the badge of the G.C.B., and various other decorations and medals, surrounded by the legend "EDWARDVS VII REX IMPERATOR." The reverse shows Britannia standing in front of the

Africa General Service Medal, 1902-1956 *(Obverse)* King Edward VII

Africa General Service Medal, 1902-1956 *(Reverse)* King Edward VII

Mark Razanauskaus Collection

British lion. Her left arm is outstretched toward the rising sun, and she holds a scroll and palm branch in her left hand. This reverse is common to all issues.

The second issue bears the bust of King George V (1910-1920), while the third issue bears the bust of Queen Elizabeth II (1952-1956).

The ribbon is yellow with black edges and two green stripes down the center. Suspension is by means of a plain, straight bar with claw mount riveted to the medal. Naming is most often in small impressed capitals, except those for the Royal Navy which were named in tall, thin, impressed capitals.

Thirty-five clasps were authorized for issue with the first medal, and an additional ten clasps were authorized for the George V issue. Only one clasp was awarded with the Queen Elizabeth II issue. ✕

Far Left—**Africa General Service Medal, 1902-1956** *(Obverse)* Queen Elizabeth II

Left—**Africa General Service Medal, 1902-1956** *(Reverse)* Queen Elizabeth II

Authorized clasps for the Africa General Service Medal, 1902-1956:

"N. Nigeria"	"East Africa 1904"	"Somaliland 1902-04 and "Jidballi" (British Regt.)
"N. Nigeria 1902"	"East Africa 1905"	
"N. Nigeria 1903"	"East Africa 1906"	"Uganda 1900"
"N. Nigeria 1903 - 04"	"East Africa 1913"	"B.C.A. 1899 - 1900"
"N. Nigeria 1904"	"East Africa 1914"	"Jubaland" (RN)
"N. Nigeria 1906"	"East Africa 1913 - 14"	"Jubaland 1917 - 18"
"S. Nigeria"	"East Africa 1915"	"Gambia"
"S. Nigeria 1902"	"East Africa 1918"	"Aro 1901 - 02"
"S. Nigeria 1902 - 03"	"West Africa 1906"	"Lango 1901"
"S. Nigeria 1903"	"West Africa 1908"	"Kissi 1905"
"S. Nigeria 1903 - 04"	"West Africa 1909 - 10"	"Nandi 1905-06"
"S. Nigeria 1904"	"Somaliland 1901"	"Shimber Berris 1914 - 15"
"S. Nigeria 1904 - 05"	"Somaliland 1902 - 04" (RN)	"Nyasaland 1915"
"S. Nigeria 1905"	"Somaliland 1908 - 10" (RN)	"Kenya" (British Regt.)—
"S. Nigeria 1905 - 06"	"Somaliland 1920" (RN)—First	21 October 1952 -
"Nigeria 1918"	time troops carried by aircraft	17 November 1956
"East Africa 1902"	carrier, H.M.S. Ark Royal	

Tibet Medal
13 December 1903–23 September 1904

This medal, authorized in February 1905, was issued in silver and bronze to those troops who were with the Tibet Mission at or beyond Silgari during the period December 1903 to September 1904. The main reason for the mission was the desire to extend trade in the north of India, as well as to counter growing Russian influence in the area. Because a good number of British patrols and expeditions had been fired upon, the result was a punitive expedition launched to teach a lesson to the upstart Tibetans.

After a number of excursions and alarms, during all of which the Tibetans were easily brushed aside, a peace treaty was signed between the British and Tibetan leadership in the Potala at Lhasa. Only one British regiment—the Royal Fusiliers—was present as a whole throughout this campaign. Approximately eight hundred and fifty silver medals were awarded to British and Indian troops, while about 2,500 native transport personnel received bronze medals.

The obverse of the medal bears the bust of King Edward VII in the uniform of a Field Marshal, with top coat, wearing the Star and Ribbon of the Order of the Garter, the badge of the G.C.B. and other medals and decorations. The surrounding legend is: "EDWARDVS VII KAISAR-I-HIND." The reverse of the medal bears a depiction of the Potala at Lhasa, with "TIBET 1903-4" below. The 1.25" wide rib-

Tibet Medal, 1903-04 *(Obverse)*

Tibet Medal *(Reverse)*

bon is red with green borders and two white stripes. Suspension is by a scroll bar with claw mount riveted to the medal. Naming of the recipient is done in engraving around the edge.

One clasp—"GYANTSE"—was granted to those who were present during the operations in and around Gyantse between 5 May 1904 and 6 July 1904 (both dates inclusive). ✕

Natal Medal
8 February 1906 – 3 August 1906

This medal was authorized and issued by the Natal Government, which refused the help of Imperial troops in putting down a rebellion by Zulu tribes. It was awarded only to Colonial troops. In February 1906, the Zulus refused to pay a British-imposed "hut tax" and murdered two policemen. Acting quickly, authorities arrested several chiefs and imposed fines upon the Zulus. In April 1906, Zulu Chief Bambata fanned smoldering discontent into flames, attacking and besieging Greytown and Eshowe.

After quickly raising troops throughout the Transvaal and Natal, several punitive columns were pushed into Zululand to pursue the rebellious natives into the forests. By early July the rebellion was crushed and the colony had been proved capable of defending itself without the intervention of Imperial troops.

Issued in silver and bronze, there were approximately 10,000 of these medals awarded—2,000 of them without a clasp. The obverse of the medal bears the head of King Edward VII, surrounded by the legend "EDWARDVS VII REX IMPERATOR." The reverse bears a representation of Natalia, with her left foot upon a native shield and weapons; her right hand holding a downward-pointing sword; and her left hand holding a branch of palm. Beside her, in a protective pose, is the figure of Britannia, holding in her left hand the Orb of Empire surmounted by a figure of Peace. The background features a hilly landscape with Kaffir kraals (native huts) and storm clouds broken by the sun.

The 1.25" wide ribbon is crimson, bordered in black, and it is attached to the medal by a plain, straight, swivel bar with ornamental claw mount attached to the medal by a rivet. The clasp has a plain raised border, and has been inscribed "1906" with a raised dot on either side. Naming of the recipient was almost always in thin block capitals. A large proportion of Natives received the decoration for their services, including over three hundred members of the Natal Native Horse. ✕

Far Left—**Natal Medal, 1906** (*Obverse*)

Left—**Natal Medal** (*Reverse*)

India General Service Medal 1908–1935

In December of 1908, a new Indian General Service Medal was authorized for the North West Frontier campaign of that year. This medal, the third in the Indian General Service series, was issued for a variety of campaigns, with most of the clasps issued for North West Frontier service, except those named for "MALABAR 1921-22" and for "BURMA 1930-32."

Although there were three different issues of this medal, the reverse was identical in every case. This was the last medal struck in the reign of Edward VII.

The obverse of the first issue is similar to the Tibet Medal, with the crowned bust of Edward VII in Field Marshal's uniform and the legend "EDWARDVS VII KAISAR-I-HIND." The second issue, which started with the medal awarded with the bar "ABOR," bears the crowned bust of King George V in robes with the inscription "GEORGIVS V KAISAR-I-HIND."

The third and final issue bears the crowned bust of George V in robes, with the legend "GEOR-GIVS . V . D . G . BRITT . OMN . REX . ET . INDIAE . IMP." This issue commenced with the clasp "NORTH WEST FRONTIER 1930-31."

The reverse bears a depiction of the fort at Jamrud, which commands the Khyber Pass, eleven miles from Peshawur. Between a "V" formed by a branch of oak and another of laurel lies a tablet with the word "INDIA." The 1.25" wide ribbon, which is green with a 0.6" wide blue stripe down the center, provides suspension for

India General Service Medal, 1908-1935 *(Obverse)*

India General Service Medal, *(Reverse)*

the medal via a floral suspension bar, as used on all of the previous India General Service Medals. This medal was struck at both the Royal Mint and the Calcutta Mint—the claw mount for the former being ornate, while the latter is plain. In both cases, the mount

is sweated to the medal. Naming varied, and is provided for each clasp issued. Holders of the medal issued after 11 August 1920, who were later mentioned in dispatches for any of the campaigns, could wear a bronze oak leaf emblem on the ribbon.

Men of the 1st Bn, Seaforth Highlanders, have a meal during the Mohand expedition, 1908. Wupperfeld collection

2nd Bn 5th Gurkha Rifles (Frontier Force) in action against Mahsuds at Anhai Tangi, 14 January 1920. Painting by Fred Roe

Authorized clasps are as follows:

"NORTH WEST FRONTIER 1908"—14 February-31 May 1908. Awarded for service in the Mohand Field Force, Bazaar Valley Field Force, and for service at Landi Kital and North of Adinazai. Named in running script.

"ABOR 1911-12"—6 October 1911-20 April 1912. First bar awarded with the second issue of this medal. Issued to British officers and Indian Troops. Naming in bold slanting script.

"AFGHANISTAN N.W.F. 1919"—6 May-8 August 1919 (12,500 clasps awarded). Awarded for service in the Third Afghan War. This was the first time the R.A.F. took part in Indian campaigns. Naming is in impressed block capitals.

"MAHSUD 1919-1920"—27 November 1919-7 May 1920. Presented to all of those who served under Major-General A. Skeen west of and including Jandola between 18 December 1919 and 8 April 1920. Also awarded to all who served with the G.O.C. Warziristan Force on the Takki Zam Line north of and including Jandola between 18 December 1919 and 8 April 1920. This clasp and the clasp for "WARZIRISTAN 1919-1921" almost always accompany one another, though medals to the Royal West Kent Regiment and the 2nd Queen Victoria's Own Sappers and Miners are known to exist with but a single bar. Naming is in thin block capitals.

"WAZIRISTAN 1919-1921"—6 May 1919-January 1921. Presented for punitive expeditions against the Tochi and Wana Wazirs and Mahsuds. These tribes had been responsible for depredations and raids since the end of the Third Afghan War. Naming is in thin, impressed block letters.

"MALABAR 1921-1922"—20 August 1921-25 February 1922. The award of this clasp was sanctioned for all troops who took part in the suppression of the Moplah Rebellion in Malabar. Naming is in thin, impressed block capitals.

"WAZIRISTAN 1921-1924"—21 December 1921-31 March 1924. Awarded to a large number of troops dispersed in small garrisons spread over a large area of North and South Waziristan and surrounding areas. Naming is in thin, impressed block capitals.

"WAZIRISTAN 1925"—9 March-1 May 1925. This clasp represents the first bar awarded solely to the R.A.F. for service in India

2nd Bn, Border Regt. on the march on the North West Frontier, 1930s.
Wupperfeld collection

Typical Waziristan tribesman from the 1920s. Note the jezal has been replaced by the British Short Lee Enfield, Mk III. Wupperfeld collection

against the Waziris and it is considered the rarest bar ever given with an India General Service Medal. Naming is done in thin, impressed block capitals, with the recipient's number, rank and name, followed by the letters "R.A.F." A total of seventy-seven officers and one hundred and ninety-eight airmen received the clasp.

"NORTH WEST FRONTIER 1930-31"—23 April 1930-22 March 1931. Awarded to all of the troops involved in any actions taken against the depredations of Abdul Ghaffar and his so-called "Redshirts" along the Mohand Frontier, as well as in the border villages. Aside from several skirmishes, action mostly involved road building. This was the first medal of the third issue, with the naming done in thin, impressed capitals.

"BURMA 1930-32"—22 December 1930-25 March 1932. Presented to all troops who were dispatched from India and who served in Burma during the period indicated. Naming is in very small block capitals.

"MOHMAND 1933"—28 July-3 October 1933. The Mohmand Column, under the command of Brigadier C.J.E. Auchinleck, operated against the Upper Mohmands. No British troops were involved. Named in small, thin, impressed block capitals.

"NORTH WEST FRONTIER 1935"—12 January-3 November 1935. Awarded to members of Mohmand Force, the R.A.F., and troops of the Peshawur, Thelum, Nowshera, and Rawalpindi Brigades. Naming is in thin, impressed block capitals. ✕

Khedive's Sudan Medal 1910

This rarely-seen medal, authorized in 1911 by the Khedive of Egypt, replaced the 1896-1908 issue. A further issue of the medal was made in 1918, bearing the new date and the cipher of the new Khedive. Between 1910 and 1922 there were a number of small revolts and uprisings, as well as one rebellion in 1916, for which this medal was awarded.

The majority of recipients of this medal were Egyptian and Sudanese troops, with the sole exception of the British officers in command. There were three clasps, "DARFUR 1916," "FASHER," and "NYIMA 1917-18" evidenced on medals presented to a small number of Army and R.A.F. personnel. (Some personnel were also awarded medals without clasps.)

The obverse of this medal bears the cipher, or inscription, of the Khedive (in this case the cipher of the new Khedive) and the date in Arabic. This reads "ABBAS HILMI THE SECOND" over the Mohammedan year "1328." The reverse depicts a lion, beautifully posed, with his front paws on a plinth, the base of which is inscribed "SUDAN," while in front of the plinth reposes a trophy of native arms. A rising sun dominates a scene of the Nile and palm trees. The 1.30" wide ribbon is black, flanked on both sides by a thin green stripe and a red outer stripe. Suspension is by a plain, straight suspender with claw mount riveted to the medal. Quite often, these medals were unnamed, although some award-

Khedive's Sudan Medal, 1910 (Obverse)

Khedive's Sudan Medal (Reverse)

ed to British troops will occasionally be found impressed in small block-style capitals. A few of the medals may also be found named in Arabic.

There were sixteen clasps authorized for this medal, with the inscription on the left done in English and the one on the right in Arabic. ✕

Clasps for Khedive's Sudan Medal, 1910, listed in chronological order:

"AWTOT"—February-April 1910

"S.KORDOFAN 1910"—10 November-19 December 1910

"SUDAN 1912"—March 1912

"ZERAF 1913-14"—December 1913-June 1914

"MANDAL'"—March 1914

"MIRI"—April 1915

"MONGALLA 1915-16"—December 1915-March 1916

"DARFUR 1916"—March-23 May 1916

"FASHER"—1 September-23 November 1916

"LAUNER—March-May 1917

"NYIMA 1917-18"—2 November 1917-February 1918

"ATWOT"—1 January-26 May 1918

"GARJAK NUER"—December 1919-April 1920

"ALIAB DINKA"—8 November 1919-May 1920

"NYALA"—26 September 1921-20 January 1922

"DARFUR"—26 September-22 November 1921

1914 Star
5 August 1914–22 November 1914

Authorized in April of 1917, the bronze 1914 Star was awarded to those who had served in France or Belgium in the period between 5 August 1914 and midnight on 22/23 November 1914. In October 1919 the King authorized the award of a clasp (the "Mons" bar) to the Star for all those who had been under fire in France or Belgium during this same time frame. Although 378,000 medals were issued, it is unknown how many included the "Mons" bar. One hundred sixty medals without bars were awarded to Canadians.

The Star has three points, with a crown replacing the topmost fourth point. At the top of the

Two members of the B.E.F. going into action at Mons, 1914. Author's collection

Members of the Royal Scots Fusiliers spread across a country road in Belgium, c. 1914. Author's collection

1914 Star *(Obverse)*

crown is a 0.5" diameter ring, stamped as part of the medal for suspension. Across the face of the Star are two crossed swords, the points and handles of which protrude between the points of the Star. On a scroll in the center is the date "1914," while immediately above and below are the months "AUG" and "NOV," with "AUG" on the top scroll. These scrolls are surrounded by a laurel wreath, at the bottom of which is a "Gv" monogram. The reverse is perfectly flat and plain, with the recipient's number, rank, name, and regiment stamped in block letters in three lines. The 1.25" wide ribbon is watered. Reading from left to right, as seen on the wearer, the colors are red, white, and blue shaded.

The "Mons" bar is bronze, with small holes at the ends to allow the bar to be stitched onto the ribbon. The legend on the bar is "5TH AUG-22nd NOV. 1914." When the medal was not worn, those entitled to the bar wore a small silver rose in the center of the ribbon. ✕

London Scotties March to the Highlands

1914-1915 Star
5 August 1914–31 December 1915

In all respects save two, the 1914-1915 Star is identical to the 1914 Star. The differences are that the medals are dated "1914-15" instead of "1914," and the months are omitted.

This medal is quite common, as some 2,366,000 were eventually issued, including 283,500 to the Royal Navy and 71,500 awarded to Canadians. The medal was issued to all those who served in a theater

Queen's gift box at Christmas, 1914, to all troops serving; usually filled with one form of tobacco or another. Author's collection

1914-1915 Star *(Obverse)*

British troops in position east of Ypres, First Battle of Ypres, 12 October–11 November 1914. Wupperfeld collection

of war between 5 August 1914 and 31 December 1915.

The Star was issued for service in France, Italy, Salonika, East and West Africa, New Guinea, the Dardanelles, the Indian Frontier, and several other theaters of war.

The ribbon for the medal is identical to that of the "1914" Star, with the reverse named in the same manner. ✕

British troops in Arras, returning from the lines in double-decker buses.
Wupperfeld collection

The Coldstream Guards, the Crack Infantrymen of Great Britain, passing through Hyde Park in Heavy Marching Order, on their Way to Paddington and the Front.

The Coldstream Guards, the Crack Infantrymen of Great Britain, passing through Hyde Park in Heavy Marching Order, on their Way to Paddington and the Front.

British War Medal 1914-1920

This medal commemorates some of the most gruesome battles in history. Casualties in the Ypres salient and at the First and Second Battle of the Somme surpassed all the British losses in World War II. When the medal was first authorized the issuance of clasps was discussed, with sixty-eight proposed for Navy participants and seventy-nine for the Army. However, these numbers proved prohibitive, and that plan was abandoned because of the great expense. Approximately 6,500,000 medals were issued in silver and bronze.

The obverse bears the coinage head of George V with the legend "GEORGIVS V BRITT: OMN: REX ET IND: IMP:." The reverse depicts St. George on horseback facing right, with the horse trampling the shield of the Central Powers. At the top is a rising sun; at the bottom is a skull and crossbones. Around the sides are the legend "1914" and "1918." The 1.25" wide ribbon is watered orange with a border of white, black, and blue stripes on each edge. Suspension is provided by means of a plain, straight, non-swiveling suspender bar with claw mount riveted to the medal.

Approximately 110,000 bronze medals were issued to Chinese, Maltese and other Native Labor Corps personnel. The medal was also issued in silver to those members of the expeditionary forces sent to Russia after the cessation of hostilities on the main battle-fields—their ostensible purpose being to guard British supplies in Russian territory. ✕

British War Medal, 1914-1920 (Obverse)

British War Medal (Reverse)

Battle of the Somme, Day One. Wupperfeld collection

Victory Medal 1914-1918

This bronze-only medal was never awarded by itself. It was issued to all those who received either the 1914 or the 1914-1915 Star, as well as—subject to certain exceptions—all those who received the British War Medal.

Eligibility required the recipient to have served with one of the fighting forces in a theater of operations between midnight 4/5 August 1914 and midnight 11/12 November 1918.

Those mentioned in dispatches between 4 August 1914 and 10 August 1920 were also authorized to wear an oak leaf on the ribbon. Approximately 5,725,000 medals were issued.

The obverse bears the full-length winged figure of Victory, a palm branch in her right hand, and her left hand extended. The reverse bears the inscription "THE GREAT WAR FOR CIVILIZATION 1914-1919" surrounded by a laurel wreath. The 1.55" wide watered ribbon is a rainbow pattern, reading from the center outwards: red, yellow, green, blue, and violet, with the colors each blending into one another. The ribbon passes through a 0.5" diameter ring, which, in turn, passes through a loop sweated to the top of the medal. Naming is in faint impressed block capital letters, and shows the number, rank, name, and unit of the recipient. There were no clasps authorized for this medal. ✕

Victory Medal, 1914-1918 *(Obverse)*

Victory Medal, 1914-1918, with Oak Leaf Cluster *(Obverse)*

Victory Medal, 1914-1918 *(Reverse)*

Territorial Force War Medal 1914–1919

The Territorial Force Medal was authorized in April 1920 for award to members of the Territorial Force, including Nursing Sisters, who, on or before 30 September 1914, had served outside the United Kingdom between the outbreak of war and the armistice, and who were ineligible for either the 1914 Star or the 1914-15 Star. A total of 33,944 of the medals were issued. This medal is worn immediately after the Allied Victory Medal and before any subsequently awarded war medals.

The obverse bears the coinage head of King George V with the legend "GEORGIVS V BRITT. OMN: REX ET IND: IMP:." The reverse bears the legend "TERRITORIAL WAR MEDAL" around the top. Inside a wreath is the inscription "FOR VOLUNTARY SERVICES OVERSEAS, 1914-19." The 1.25" wide ribbon is watered yellow with two green stripes. The medal is suspended on a plain, non-swiveling suspender. Naming is in impressed block capitals. No clasps were authorized for use with this medal. ✕

Far Left—**Territorial Force War Medal, 1914-1919** *(Obverse)*

Left—**Territorial Force War Medal, 1914-1919** *(Reverse)*

The General Service Medal
1918-1964

This medal was instituted 19 January 1923 to be awarded for services other than on the adjacent frontiers of India and East, West, or Central Africa. The General Service Medal is appropriate for minor campaigns that did not justify a separate medal. Due to the number of skirmishes and engagements undertaken in the period covered, it is virtually impossible to determine the total number of medals issued.

The medal has been issued with three separate effigies and several different legends on the obverse. The issues are as follows:

1st Issue (1918-1934)—The coinage head of King George V facing left and the legend "GEORGIVS V BRITT :OMN :REX ET IND :IMP."

2nd Issue (1934-1936)—The crowned head of King George V in robes and the legend "GEORGIVS V .D .G BRITT .OMN .REX .ET .INDAE .IMP."

3rd Issue (1936-1949)—The crowned head of King George VI and the legend "GEORGIVS VI D :G :BR :OMN :REX ET INDAE IMP:."

4th Issue (1949-1952)—The crowned head of King George VI and the legend "GEORGIVS VI DEI GRA :BRITT :OMN :REX FID :DEF+."

5th Issue (1952-1953)—The crowned bust of Queen Elizabeth II and the legend "ELIZABETH II D. G :BR :OMN :REGINA F.D. +."

6th Issue (1953-1962) - The crowned bust of Queen Elizabeth II and the legend "ELIZABETH II DEI GRATIA REGINA F. D. +."

The reverse of the medal bears the standing, winged figure of

The General Service Medal, 1918-1964, bar "Kurdistan" *(Obverse)*

The General Service Medal, 1918-1964 *(Reverse)*

Victory, who is placing a wreath over the emblems of the Army and the Royal Air force with her right hand, while holding a trident in her left hand. The 1.25" wide ribbon is purple with a 0.35" wide centered green stripe. Suspension is by an ornate ornamental suspender which, in the case of the first two issues, does not swivel. A floral claw mount attached to the suspender is sweated onto the medal. Those mentioned in dis-

patches during any of the campaigns for which the medal was awarded are entitled to wear an oak leaf emblem on the ribbon.

Sixteen clasps were authorized for this medal, as follows:

"S. PERSIA"—12 November 1918-22 June 1919. Presented for operations near Bushire and Banda Abbas in 1918 and 1919.

"KURDISTAN"—23 May 1919-6 December 1919, and from 19

The General Service Medal, 1918-1964, Queen Elizabeth II "For Campaign Service" *(Reverse)*

March-18 June 1923. Awarded for peace-keeping operations and various skirmishes in 1919 and 1923. The situation in 1923 is significant in that it marked the first time troops were airlifted for a military operation.

"IRAQ"—10 December 1919-17 November 1920. Issued for taking part in the suppression of an Arab rebellion in the Iraqi countryside during 1919 and 1920.

"N.W. PERSIA"—10 August-31 December 1920. This clasp was prersented to members of the North Persia Force (known as Noperforce), as well as to those on lines of communication.

"SOUTHERN DESERT, IRAQ"—8 January-3 June 1928. This clasp, awarded primarily to the R.A.F., was for service against the Akhwan in the Southern Desert of Iraq.

"NORTHERN KURDISTAN"—15 March-21 June 1932. This clasp was issued with the George V obverse to Iraqi levies and the R.A.F. for operations against Shaik Admed of Barzan.

"PALESTINE"—19 April 1936-3 September 1939. This medal and the following five medals were issued with the crowned coinage head of George VI and the small raised rim common to this issue. The medal was awarded to all those involved in suppressing the Arab revolt in Palestine.

"S.E. ASIA 1945-46"—This clasp was issued to those members of the service for post-war operations in Java, Sumatra, and French Indo-China.

"BOMB AND MINE CLEARANCE 1945-49" and "BOMB AND MINE CLEARANCE 1945-56"—This clasp is reasonably self-explanatory. Eligibility originally required one hundred and eighty days of active duty in bomb and mine clearance in the United Kingdom and Northern Ireland. However, the period was extended to 1 January 1955 and included service in the Mediterranean.

"PALESTINE 1945-48"—27 September 1945-30 June 1948. This clasp will be found with either the third or fourth issue

New Zealand troops on patrol in the jungles of Malaysia.
Author's collection

Preparation for a patrol into the Rhadfan. Wupperfeld collection

obverse. It was issued to all British personnel involved in the upheavals in Palestine prior to the birth of the state of Israel.

"MALAYA"—16 June 1948-31 July 1960 (Colony of Singapore 16 June 1948-31 January 1959). This clasp will be found with either the third or the fourth issue obverse. It was awarded to personnel of the British Army, the R.A.F., Local Forces, Civil Police Forces and certain civilians who were involved in Anti-Communist operations in the Colony of Singapore and the Federation of Malaya.

"CYPRUS"—1 April 1955-19 April 1959. Presented to British Army and R.A.F. personnel for operations in Cyprus between the dates indicated.

British Commonwealth troops under attack by Indonesian troops in North Borneo. Wupperfeld collection

A British
Regimental sniper
in action in
South Yemen.
Wupperfeld collection

General Service Medal, First Issue,
bar "S. Persia"

General Service Medal, First Issue,
bar "N.W. Persia"

"NEAR EAST"—31 October-22 December 1956. Issued to service personnel involved in the Suez Canal landings in 1956, either in Egypt or off the Egyptian coast.

"ARABIAN PENINSULAR"—1 January 1957-30 June 1960. This clasp was authorized for issue to those with thirty days of service in the Aden Colony or Protectorate, the Sultanates of Muscat or Oman, and any of the Gulf States. Those who received a mention in dispatches or a Queen's commendation were entitled to affix an oak leaf emblem on the ribbon.

"BRUNEI"—8-23 December 1962. Presented to all service personnel involved in operations in Brunei, North Borneo, and Sarawak in December 1962.

"NORTHERN IRELAND"— Awarded to all service personnel who served in Northern Ireland during the ongoing troubles. ✕

General Service Medal, First Issue, bar "Kurdistan" *(Obverse)*

General Service Medal, First Issue *(Reverse)*

General Service Medal, First Issue, bar "Iraq" *(Obverse)*

General Service Medal, First Issue, bar "Southern Desert, Iraq" *(Obverse)*

General Service Medal, Third Issue, bar "Palestine" *(Obverse)*

General Service Medal, Third Issue, bar "S.E.Asia 1945-46" *(Obverse)*

General Service Medal, Third Issue, bar "Palestine 1945-48" *(Obverse)*

General Service Medal, Fourth Issue, bar "Malaya" *(Obverse)*

General Service Medal, Fifth Issue, bar "Malaya" *(Obverse)*

Campaign Service Medal, Sixth Issue, bar "Cyprus" *(Obverse)*

Campaign Service Medal, Sixth Issue, bar "South Arabia" *(Obverse)*

Campaign Service Medal, Sixth Issue, "For Campaign Service" *(Reverse)*

Campaign Service Medal, Sixth Issue, bar "Near East" *(Obverse)*

Campaign Service Medal, Sixth Issue, bars "Radfan", "South Arabia," and "Northern Ireland" *(Reverse)*

Campaign Service Medal, Sixth Issue, bar "Arabian Peninsula" *(Obverse)*

Left—**Campaign Service Medal, Sixth Issue, bar "Brunei"** *(Reverse)*

Center—**Campaign Service Medal, Sixth Issue, bar "Northern Ireland"** *(Obverse)*

Right—**Campaign Service Medal, Sixth Issue, showing unusual backing and suspension** *(Reverse).*

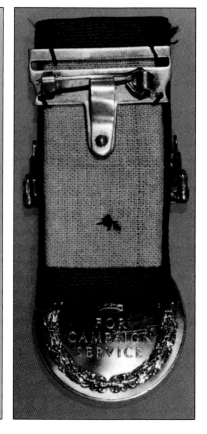

India General Service Medal 1936-1939

This medal was instituted on 3 August 1938. It replaced the India General Service Medal, 1908, which was used during the reigns of King Edward VII and King George V. This was the fourth, and the final, award in the I.G.S.M. series. The accession of King George VI to the throne was deemed a most convenient time to redesign the entire medal instead of merely re-doing the obverse.

The obverse bears the crowned coinage head of King George VI and the legend "GEORGIVS VI D:G:BR:OMN:REX ET INDIAE IMP:." The reverse presents the depiction of a tiger with raised paws, standing on a small, rocky hillock. The tiger's head is turned toward the back, almost meeting its tail, which is curved over the animal's back. The word "INDIA" is seen above, while the remainder of the reverse is plain. The 1.25" wide ribbon is green with a 0.65" gray sandy-colored center, separated from the green by two red stripes.

Suspension is by an ornate floral suspender—similar to former India Model patterns—with two different styles of claw mount. The medal was struck at both the London and Calcutta Mints. The London version of the medal is more artistic and has an ornamental claw mount, while the medal struck in India is more crudely done and has just a simple claw mount.

Naming to this medal is in thin, impressed capitals.

Two bars were authorized for issue with the medal; they are as follows:

India General Service Medal, 1936-1939 *(Obverse)*

India General Service Medal *(Reverse)*

"NORTH WEST FRONTIER 1936-37"—24 November 1936-16/17 January 1937, and 16/17 January 1937-15/16 December 1937. Issued to all personnel involved in operations in Waziristan during the dates shown, inclusive.

"NORTH WEST FRONTIER 1937-1939"—15/16 December 1937-31 December 1939; 15/16 June

1938-1/2 November 1938; 31 December 1938-31 January 1939; and 31 December 1939-1 January 1940. Sanctioned for all personnel involved in operations in Waziristan during the dates indicated.

Recipients of a mention in dispatches were entitled to wear an oak leaf emblem in the ribbon. ✕

1939-1945 Star
3 September 1939–15 August 1945

British troops sharing smokes with a French Marine during a commando raid on Norway. Wupperfeld collection

1939-1945 Star *(Obverse)*

The 1939-1945 Star was considered the "qualifying medal" in a series of eight campaign stars awarded for service during World War II. Those entitled to this star were eligible for the others upon entering the applicable theater of operations—except in the case of the Atlantic, Air Crew Europe and Africa Stars. This Star covered service in World War II between 3 September 1939 and 2 September 1945. All of the stars in the series were of similar design, and made of a yellow copper zinc alloy in the form of a six-pointed star.

The shape of the stars is similar to those awarded for service in the 1843 Gwalior Campaign. In the star's center is the Royal Cipher, surmounted by a crown superimposed upon a circle that displays the title of the star. The reverse is plain, for, based upon a penny-pinching decision by the Honours Committee, it was determined that campaign stars and medals awarded to Imperial Troops for service during World War II would not be stamped with the recipient's information at government expense. However, permission was granted to add the information by private arrangement. Thus, the value of the individual medal or of a group is lowered, and the authenticity of any named group should be very carefully verified.

The 1.25" wide ribbon has three equal-width stripes of dark blue, red, and light blue, and suspension is by means of a ring which is fastened to the uppermost point of the star. ×

The Atlantic Star
3 September 1939–8 May 1945

The Atlantic Star *(Obverse)*

This Star was awarded to commemorate the battle of the Atlantic. Six months of service afloat constituted the required qualifying period The majority of these medals were awarded to personnel of the Royal Navy and the Merchant Navy. However, R.A.F. and Army personnel who had attached service with the Royal Navy or the Merchant Navy qualified for the award in the same manner as members of the parent service with which they served.

If a recipient of this award also qualified for the France and Germany Star, he could wear a small silver rose emblem on the ribbon of the star first earned.

In the center of the star is the Royal Cipher, surmounted by a crown superimposed upon a circle that displays the title of the star: "THE ATLANTIC STAR" in The 1.25" wide ribbon is a shaded and watered dark blue, white, and sea green, with the colors running into one another. Suspension is in the customary manner of the star awards, and the reverse of the star is left unmarked. ✕

The Africa Star
10 June 1940–12 May 1943

Award of this star required one or more days of service in North Africa between 10 June 1940 and 12 May 1943, both dates inclusive.

In the center of the star is the Royal Cipher, surmounted by a crown that is superimposed upon a circle displaying the title of the star—in this case "THE AFRICA STAR." The reverse, in keeping with the series, is blank. The 1.25" wide ribbon is pale buff with a central red stripe and two narrow stripes—one of dark blue, and the

Typical tank crew, North Africa. Wupperfeld collection

The Africa Star *(Obverse)*

other of pale blue. The dark blue stripe is to the left when facing the wearer.

Three emblems were awarded to the Army, consisting of:

(1) The numeral "8" which represented the "Eighth Army" was awarded for service in the Eighth Army between 23 October 1942 (the date of the battle of El Alamein) and 12 May 1943.

(2) The numeral "1" representing the "First Army" was awarded for service in the First Army in a unit or formation in Tunis or Algeria between 8 November and 31 December 1942, or thereafter between 1 January and 12 May 1943 in any unit under the command of the First Army.

(3) The silver rose emblem was awarded to personnel of the Headquarters of the 18th Army Group who did not qualify for either of the numerals. Members of the Union Defence Force attached to the South African Air Force Squadrons, which qualified for the rose emblem, were also eligible for it.

Only one bar, or emblem, was awarded to any individual in conjunction with this star. If, however, an individual qualified for all three bars, then the one to which he first became entitled was awarded.

When the star is worn, the appropriate bar inscribed with the title "Eighth Army," "First Army," or "North Africa 1942-43" is worn attached to the ribbon. ✕

Members of an S.A.S. patrol returning from three months behind enemy lines in North Africa.
Wupperfeld collection

Survivors of an engagement in North Africa.
Wupperfeld collection

The Pacific Star
8 December 1941 – 2 September 1945

The Pacific Star *(Obverse)*

This medal was awarded for service in the Pacific theater between 8 December 1941 and 2 September 1945. In the case of the Army, there was no prior time qualification, while Air Force and Navy personnel were required to have completed at least a single operational sortie over the appropriate land or sea area to qualify for the award.

Qualifying service for the Army was restricted to territory that had been subjected to enemy or allied invasion. Service in Burma was excluded; however, service in China and/or Malaya between 8 December 1941 and 15 February 1942 was included.

In the center of the star is the Royal Cipher, surmounted by a crown superimposed upon a circle that displays the title of the star, in this case "THE PACIFIC STAR." In keeping with the full series, the reverse is plain. The 1.25" wide ribbon is dark green with red edges and a central yellow stripe, and includes a thin stripe of dark blue and another of light blue.

Those qualifying for both the Pacific Star and the Burma Star were also awarded a silver rose emblem to be worn on the ribbon of the star that was acquired first. The recipient of a Pacific Star who also qualified for the Burma Star was awarded a bar with the title "Burma" to be affixed to the ribbon when only the Pacific Star medal was being worn. ✕

The Burma Star
11 December 1941 – 2 September 1945

Orde Wingate's Chindits at a river crossing in Burma, c. 1944.
Wupperfeld collection

The Burma Star *(Obverse)*

This star was awarded for Burma Campaign service between 11 December 1941 and 2 September 1945. For land operations, the award was made for service in Burma and for service on land in Assam, east of the Brahmaputra. Service in China and Malaya between 16 February 1942 and 2 September 1945 was included.

In the center of the star is the Royal Cipher, which is surmounted by a crown superimposed upon a circle that displays the title of the star: "THE BURMA STAR." In keeping with the full series, the reverse is plain. The 1.25" wide ribbon is dark blue with a wide central red stripe; the two blue borders each have orange stripes running up their middles. The red is symbolic of Commonwealth Forces and the orange symbolizes the sun.

Those qualifying for both the Burma Star and the Pacific Star received a silver rose emblem to be worn on the ribbon of the star that was acquired first. The recipient of a Burma Star who also qualified for the Pacific Star was awarded a bar with the title "Pacific," to be affixed to the ribbon when only the Burma Star was being worn. ✕

The Italy Star
11 June 1943–8 May 1945

This star was awarded for operational service in Sicily or Italy from the date of the capture of the island of Pantellaria on 11 June 1943 to 8 May 1945. For the Army, there was no prior time qualification. Service in the Mediterranean and the Aegean Seas and operations in and around the Dodecanese, Corsica, Greece, Sardinia and Yugoslavia after 11 June 1943 would qualify an individual for this star.

If they did not subsequently serve in another operational area, those who entered those last five specified areas after 8 November 1944 would qualify for the Italy Star, but not for the 1939-45 Star. Entry into Austrian Territory during the last few days of the war qualified one for the Italy Star, but not for the France and Germany Star. The Italy Star was awarded in addition to the other stars, so there were no clasps.

In the center of the star is the Royal Cipher, surmounted by a crown superimposed upon a circle that displays the title of the star—"THE ITALY STAR" in this case. In keeping with the rest of the series, the reverse is plain. The 1.25" wide ribbon represents the Italian flag colors, arranged as red, white, green, white, and red in equal-width stripes. ✕

The Italy Star (*Obverse*)

British troops mopping up Umbertide on the River Tiber, in the Italian campaign.
Wupperfeld collection.

The France and Germany Star
6 June 1944–8 May 1945

This star was awarded for service in France, Belgium, Holland, or Germany between D-Day and the surrender of Germany (6 June 1944 to 8 May 1945). For the Army, qualification required participation in any operation on land in any of the above counties.

This star was not awarded in addition to the Atlantic and Air Crew Europe Star. Therefore, when the ribbon alone was worn, a silver rose emblem was awarded to be worn on the ribbon of the star first earned. Those who qualified for the Atlantic, Air Crew Europe, or France and Germany Star, or two of them, were awarded only the star for which they first qualified. The bar "Atlantic" was awarded to be worn on the ribbon to indicate that service had been rendered that would have qualified the recipient for the second star. A second bar was not awarded to those who qualified for all three stars. Note: a bar "Air Crew Europe" was not awarded with this star.

In the center of the star is the Royal Cipher surmounted by a crown superimposed upon a circle that displays the title of the star, in this case "THE FRANCE AND GERMANY STAR." In keeping with the series, the reverse is plain. The 1.25" wide ribbon bears the colors blue, white, red, white, and blue in equal width stripes, symbolic of the Union flag, as well as the flags of France and The Netherlands. Belgium is not represented in these colors. ✕

The France and Germany Star *(Obverse)*

British troops on Normandy's beaches, D-day, 1944. Sgt. Mapham

The Defence Medal
3 September 1939-15 August 1945

In general, the Defence Medal in cupro-nickel was awarded for three years of service in Great Britain until 8 May 1945, or for six months service overseas in territories subjected to air attacks or closely threatened. In the case of mine and bomb disposal units, the time qualification was three months.

To qualify for the award of this medal, it was necessary to have served in Great Britain from 3 September 1939 to 8 May 1945, or overseas until the end of all hostilities in the Pacific, 15 August 1945. Civil Defence Services in military operational areas subject to enemy air attack were included for eligibility, as were these services when they were employed in other areas of the Commonwealth, or the Colonial Empire, subject to comparable conditions. Service in the West Indies or in West Africa did not qualify.

The obverse of the medal bears the uncrowned effigy of King George VI and the legend "GEORGIVS VI: BR: OMN: REX F: D: IND: IMP." The reverse depicts the Royal Crown resting upon the stump of an oak tree, flanked by two lions. At the top left is the date "1939," while at top right appears "1945." "THE DEFENCE MEDAL" appears in the exergue. The 1.25" ribbon is

The Defence Medal *(Obverse)*

The Defence Medal *(Reverse)*

flame colored with green edges, symbolizing enemy attacks upon the green island of Great Britain. The black-out is commemorated by two thin black stripes down

the center of the green stripes. Suspension is by a plain, straight, non-swiveling suspender. The medal was unnamed, and there were no clasps authorized. ✕

The War Medal
3 September 1939 – 2 September 1945

This cupro-nickel medal was awarded to all full-time personnel of all the Armed Forces, regardless of where their wartime service was actually rendered. Operational and non-operational service counted, providing that it was of twenty-eight days or more in duration.

Operational service that was terminated by death, wounds, or a disability due to service, capture, or the cessation of hostilities that qualified for a Campaign Star also qualified the recipient for the War Medal, even if the total service term did not amount to twenty-eight days. However, this proviso did not apply to those who were not awarded one of the Campaign Stars. If one of the Campaign Stars was awarded for service of less than twenty-eight days, the War Medal was granted in addition.

The obverse of the medal bears the crowned head of King George VI surrounded by the legend "GEORGIVS VI D: G: BR: OMB: REX ET INDIAE IMP:". The reverse depicts a lion atop a dragon supine on its back, with the lion's paw resting upon the dragon's raised head. The 1.25" wide ribbon embodies the red, white, and blue colors of the Union Jack. A narrow red stripe runs down the center, and it is flanked by a narrow white stripe on either side. These white stripes are, in turn,

The War Medal *(Obverse)*

The War Medal *(Reverse)*

flanked by blue stripes, while the outside edges of the ribbon are red. Suspension is by means of a plain, straight, non-swiveling suspender. The medal was issued unnamed.

The War Medal may also carry one bronze oak leaf signifying that the recipient has been mentioned in dispatches, irrespective of the theater of war, or the number of times mentioned. ✕

India Service Medal 68 1939–45

This cupro-nickel medal was sanctioned in 1946 to be awarded to Indian Forces officers and men for service in the period between September 1939 and September 1945. The basic qualification for this award was three years' non-operational service in India or elsewhere.

This medal (220,000 issued) was awarded in addition to the various campaign stars and the War Medal of 1939-45, but was not issued to those who qualified for the Defence Medal of 1939-45. All ranks of the Indian Forces, as well as serving British officers and other ranks, were entitled to the award, including Reserve, State, and Women's forces.

The obverse of the medal is the same as that of the War Medal. The reverse depicts a relief map of India with the word "INDIA" above and the dates "1939-45" below. The 1.25" wide ribbon is dark blue with a thin light blue stripe down the center. This center stripe is flanked by wider parallel light blue stripes on each side. The light blue is that of the ribbon of the Order of the Star of India, while the dark blue represents the ribbon of the Order of the Indian Empire. Suspension is by means of a plain, straight, non-swiveling suspender, with a claw mount riveted to the medal. The medal was issued unnamed. ✕

Far Left—**India Service Medal** (*Obverse*)

Left—**India Service Medal** (*Reverse*)
Loren Schave Collection

Canadian Volunteer Service Medal 1939–45

This medal was issued in 1943, by sanction, in silver only. Basic qualification for the award was eighteen months voluntary service in the Canadian armed forces or other recognized organizations between September 1939 and March 1947. The later closing date was to ensure that those serving on 1 September 1945 would qualify upon completion of eighteen months of uninterrupted active service. Approximately one million medals were issued.

The obverse face of the medal depicts seven marching figures which represent the three fighting services, male and female, together with the Nursing Service. Around the circumference at top is the inscription "1939 CANADA 1945," while along the bottom portion is "VOLUNTARY SERVICE VOLONTAIRE." On the reverse is the Canadian Coat of Arms. The 1.25" wide ribbon is, from edge to edge: green, scarlet, royal blue, scarlet, and green. Suspension of the medal is by means of a small ring, formed as part of the medal, through which passes another, larger ring. This larger ring, in turn, passes through a hole in the center of a straight, non-swiveling suspender of somewhat unusual design. These medals were issued unnamed.

There are no bars to commemorate any particular actions or theaters of operation, but a straight bar with a maple leaf emblem in the center was issued to denote service outside the Dominion of Canada. ✕

Canadian Volunteer Service Medal *(Obverse)*

Canadian Volunteer Service Medal *(Reverse)* Loren Schave Collection

Africa Service Medal 1939–45

This medal (190,000 issued) was sanctioned in 1943 and awarded to South African Forces personnel who served in the Second World War. The basic qualification for this award was the signing of an oath to serve in the Union forces in Africa or overseas. Full-time service of thirty or more days qualified the recipient for the award.

The obverse of the medal bears the map of Africa, with the circumference inscribed "AFRICAN SERVICE MEDAL" along the left half and "AFRIKADIENS-MEDALJE" along the right half. The reverse bears the depiction of a leaping springbok, facing right. The 1.25" wide ribbon is mostly orange, with one green and one gold stripe on each edge. Suspension is by means of a plain, straight suspender with claw mount riveted to the medal. The medals are usually named in small impressed capitals with the number and the name of the recipient. The prefix "N" indicates a Native, while the prefix "C" indicates a Colored recipient.

When a recipient has received mention in dispatches, the medal is issued with a small bronze Protea leaf emblem for attachment to the ribbon. ✕

Africa Service Medal *(Obverse)*

Africa Service Medal *(Reverse)*
Loren Schave Collection

Australia Service Medal 1939-45

On the first day of December 1949, the Prime Minister of Australia announced the King's approval of a medal to be awarded to all members of the Australian armed forces who had served overseas for at least eighteen months between 3 September 1939 and 2 September 1945, or who had served three years at home. Service which was terminated by death, injury, or capture automatically qualified one for the award. About 177,000 medals in nickel-silver were issued.

The obverse of the medal bears the crowned effigy of King George VI, while the reverse bears the Coat of Arms of the Commonwealth of Australia. The 1.25" wide ribbon is dark blue, khaki, and light blue with intervening stripes of red. The first three colors represent the Navy, Army, and Air Force respectively, while the red stripes represent the Australian Merchant Marine. Suspension is accomplished by means of a plain, straight, non-swiveling suspender with claw mount riveted to the medal. The medal was usually named in impressed capitals, showing the recipient's number and name. The prefix of the number denotes the state in which the recipient enlisted. There were no clasps authorized for this medal. ✕

Far Left—**Australia Service Medal** *(Obverse)*

Left—**Australia Service Medal** *(Reverse)*

Steve Johnson Collection

New Zealand War Service Medal 1939-45

Approximately 238,000 cupro-nickel medals were issued to all members of the New Zealand forces who served during the Second World War and completed one month of full-time service or six months of part-time service. The period to qualify for this award was from 3 September 1939 to 2 September 1945. In addition to the regular forces, many Reserve and Home Guard units were also entitled to this medal. Termination of service caused by death, injury, or capture resulted in automatic award of the medal.

The obverse of the medal displays the uncrowned head of King George VI, while the reverse bears the inscription "FOR SERVICE TO NEW ZEALAND 1939-45" above a frond of ferns. The 1.25" wide ribbon is watered black, and edged with white stripes 3/16" wide. Suspension is by means of a distinctive and somewhat elaborate suspender formed from two fern leaves which are joined at the stalk end to form a "V." The tips of the leaves are joined by a thin bar to accommodate the ribbon. The medals were issued unnamed, and no clasps were authorized. ✕

Right—**New Zealand War Service Medal** *(Obverse)*

Far Right—**New Zealand War Service Medal** *(Obverse)*
Loren Schave Collection

South Africa Medal for War Service 1939–46

South Africa Medal for War Service *(Obverse)*

South Africa Medal for War Service *(Obverse)*
Steve Johnson Collection

This silver medal was instituted by Royal Warrant dated 29 December 1946 for award to both men and women, whether or not they were British citizens, for services rendered between September 1939 and February 1946. The main qualifications were two years of service in an official voluntary organization in South Africa or elsewhere. At least one year had to be continual service and, additionally, the work had to be voluntary and unpaid.

The obverse bears the South African Union Coat of Arms, while the reverse displays a wreath of Protea which encircles the dates "1939-1945." The words "SOUTH AFRICA-SUID-AFRICA-FOR WAR SERVICES-VIR OORLOGS-DIENSTE" appear along the circumference. The ribbon is divided into three equal-width, vertical stripes of orange, white, and blue,

as read from left when facing the wearer. Suspension is effected by a plain, straight suspender with claw mount riveted to the medal. The medal was issued unnamed, and no clasps were authorized.

The medal could also be issued with a bronze Protea leaf emblem. This emblem was attached to the ribbon to denote a mention made in dispatches or the receipt of a commendation from the King. ✕

Southern Rhodesian War Service Medal 1939–45

74

Southern Rhodesian War Service Medal
(Obverse)

Southern Rhodesian War Service Medal
(Reverse) Steve Johnson Collection

This is a very scarce cupronickel medal—only 1,700 having been issued. It was awarded only to those who served in Southern Rhodesia at any time during the hostilities. Members of a service who qualified for a campaign star or medal were not eligible for this medal. Because such a large proportion of the armed forces served overseas in this period, relatively few of this particular medal were ever awarded—hence its rarity.

The obverse bears the crowned head of George VI surrounded by the inscription "GEORGIVS VI D: G: BR: OMN: REX ET INDIAE IMP:." The reverse face bears the arms of Southern Rhodesia surrounded by "FOR SERVICE IN SOUTHERN RHODESIA 1939-1945." The 1.25" wide ribbon is dark green with narrow black and red stripes at each edge. Suspension is accomplished by means of a plain, straight suspender with a claw mount riveted to the medal.

This medal was issued unnamed, and no clasps were authorized. ✕

The Korea Medal
2 July 1950–10 June 1953

This medal was sanctioned by King George VI in 1951 for award to members of British and Commonwealth forces who participated in operations in Korea on behalf of the United Nations between 2 July 1950 and 10 June 1953. One day of service in Korea qualified personnel from all of the services. All issues of the medal are in cupro-nickel, with the exception of the Canadian (27,000 issued), which is .800 silver.

The British and Commonwealth forces sent to Korea were small in comparison to American forces which served there. However, the Commonwealth Division saw very

Guns of the 2nd Regt., RCHA in action, June 1951, Korea. Wupperfeld collection

The Korea Medal, 1950-1853 *(Obverse)*

The Korea Medal *(Reverse)*

The Korea Medal, Canada, 1950-1853 *(Obverse)*

The Korea Medal, Canada, *(Reverse)*

heavy and extensive fighting, especially troops of the Gloucestershire Regiment who participated in the epic fight on Hill 235 at the Imjin River. Of seven hundred and fifty members of the 1st Battalion, forty managed to fight their way back to their own lines, while one hundred and fifty men held the hill until relieved. The remaining men were either killed or captured.

There were two issues of this medal. The obverse bears the laureate bust of Queen Elizabeth II facing right, surrounded by a legend that on the first issue read "ELIZABETH II DEI GRA: BRITT: OMN: REGINA F: D" and on the second, scarcer issue, "ELIZABETH II: DEI: GRATIA: REGINA F: D:+." Medals to Canadian Forces show "CANADA" under the bust. The reverse depicts Hercules, armed with a dagger, with his left arm extended out horizontally holding Hydra, which he is also holding off with his left leg. The word "KOREA" is in the exergue. The 1.25" wide ribbon is yellow, with two 0.25" wide blue stripes. Suspension is by a plain, straight, non-swiveling suspender. Naming is in thin impressed capitals.

A single bronze oak leaf emblem is awarded for wear on the ribbon for those mentioned in dispatches. ✕

Men of "B," RAR firing from slit trenches, Korea.
Wupperfeld collection

2nd PPCLI attacking point 419, 24 February 51, Korea.
Wupperfeld collection

The last stand of the Glosters, with "Drummie" Buss playing regimental calls in the foreground.
Wupperfeld collection

The United Nations Service Medal
27 June 1950–27 July 1953

This medal was instituted by the General Assembly of the United Nations on 12 December 1950 in "recognition of the valour and sacrifice of the men and women who have served on behalf of the United Nations in repelling the aggression in Korea." The full title of the medal is the "United Nations Service Medal, with clasp 'KOREA,' for service in Defence of the Principles of the Charter of the United Nations." This would lead one to believe that the medal was to be a general service award, with more clasps possible for future U.N. military campaigns. The award of the Korea Medal automatically ensured the award of the U.N. Service Medal.

The obverse of this circular medal bears the emblem of the United Nations, which is a polar projection map of the world, encircled by two olive branches—the traditional symbol of peace. The reverse is plain except for the five-line inscription "FOR SERVICE IN DEFENCE OF THE PRINCIPLES OF THE CHARTER OF THE UNITED NATIONS."

The 1.25" wide unwatered ribbon displays nine blue and eight white stripes. Suspension is by a plain, straight, non-swiveling suspender with claw mount made to appear to be riveted to the medal. The suspender has a narrow bar above over which the ribbon pass-

The United Nations Service Medal
(Obverse)

The United Nations Service Medal
(Reverse)

es—all components of the suspension device, and an inscribed upper bar being struck as one piece. The medal is unnamed, except to Canadians, which have the recipient's number and name on the rim.

Of particular interest is the fact that this medal was made in the following languages: Amharic, Dutch, English, French, Greek, Italian, Korean, Spanish, Thai, Turkic, Tagalog, and Flemish. ✕

Vietnam Medal 1964

This award was sanctioned in 1965, with terms of the Royal Warrant restricting issuance of the medal to members of the Australian armed forces who served in Vietnam after 28 May 1964. By these conditions, it was possible for a man to be awarded both this medal and the Campaign Service Medal where his tour of duty overlaped the qualifying date. The period of service necessary to obtain the award was one day on land, twenty-eight days at sea, or thirty days on an official visit.

The obverse bears the crowned bust of Queen Elizabeth, facing right, surrounded by the legend "ELIZABETH II DEI GRATIA REGINA F.D." The reverse face displays a symbolic representation of the ideological war in Vietnam, showing a naked figure separating two spheres of influence—the left hand pushing away one sphere, while the right hand protects the other shielded by his back. Above the head of the figure, in the curve of the medal, is the word "VIETNAM." The ribbon is dark blue, light blue, red, and yellow striped, representing the colors of the three services and the national colors of the Republic of Vietnam. Suspension is by means of an ornate, non-swiveling suspender with claw mount sweated to the medal.

This medal was the first to be designed and produced in Australia. When issued, it was

Vietnam Medal *(Obverse)*

Vietnam Medal *(Reverse)*

named in one of two possible styles. Australian troops received their medals impressed in large capitals, while medals for New Zealand forces were impressed in small capitals. Australian troops were awarded 18,000 medals, and 4,000 medals were issued to New Zealand forces. No clasps were authorized for this medal. ✕

South Vietnam Service Medal 1964

This medal was issued by the South Vietnamese government to Australian and New Zealand troops for operations recognized by award of the Vietnam Medal. Basic qualification for issue of the Service Medal was six months of service in Vietnam. This medal is usually accompanied by the Vietnam Medal, although the Vietnam Medal could be earned without the recipient receiving the South Vietnam Service Medal.

The obverse of the medal bears, in the center, a black enameled circle, outlined in gold, within which a map of Vietnam appears with red flames bursting from its center. This circle is centered upon a gold-bordered and white-enameled six-point star. Between the arms of the star golden rays are emitted. The reverse is relatively plain, with the exception of a Vietnamese inscription which appears in the center. The ribbon is white and edged in green, with two equal-width green stripes running its length.

The medal is attached to its ribbon by a three-piece loop arrangement, one component of which is attached to the uppermost point of the star; another through which the ribbon is passed; and a third ring linking the other two.

Originally, these medals were manufactured in Vietnam and were quite crude. The Australians took over the manufacture of the medal and began to name them on the reverse with the number and name of the recipient. There were no clasps for this medal. ✕

Right—**South Vietnam Campaign Medal** (*Obverse*)

Far Right—**South Vietnam Campaign Medal** (*Reverse*)

The South Atlantic Medal
1982

The South Atlantic Medal, 1982, with Campaign Service Medal, bar "North Ireland" (*Obverse*)

pproximately 20,000 cupro-nickel "Falklands Campaign" medals were awarded for service involving the recapture of the Falkland Islands in the South Atlantic from Argentinian armed forces. Basic qualifications included: (1) Service of one day or more in the Falkland Islands, or in their Dependencies, or in the South Atlantic south of 35-degrees South and north of 60-degrees South, or in any operational aircraft sortie south of Ascension Island; and (2) Thirty days or more of service—

not necessarily continuous—in an area of the South Atlantic south of 7-degrees South and north of 35-degrees South. If qualifying service was brought to an end before the completion of the specified time on account of death, capture, wounding, or other service-related disability, the award was granted.

The obverse bears the crowned effigy of Queen Elizabeth II looking right, and surrounded by the inscription "ELIZABETH II DEI GRATIA REGINA FID. DEI." The reverse bears the Coat-of-Arms of

the Falkland Islands, the shield divided horizontally by a wavy line, with the upper part depicting a ram standing on grasses, while below that is an illustration of the ship "DESIRE." Under the ship is the Island's motto, "DESIRE THE RIGHT." Beneath the shield and motto are laurel fronds joining at the base, while above the shield is inscribed "SOUTH ATLANTIC MEDAL." The ribbon is blue, shading to white, shading to a central green stripe, and suspension of the medal is by means of a straight, plain bar with an ornate claw mount as part of the top of the medal.

Those recipients who qualified under part (1) of the qualification requirements were permitted to wear a distinguishing silver floral rosette emblem on the ribbon of the medal. There were no clasps authorized for this medal. ✕

British 5th Infantry AA gunner, Falkland Islands.
Wupperfeld collection

British machine gunner, Falkland Islands. Wupperfeld collection

The Gulf War Medal 1991

The official British campaign medal sanctioned for operations in the Persian Gulf was announced to Parliament by the Prime Minister in August of 1991. Qualifications for receipt of the medal include:

(1) Thirty days service continuously between 2 August 1990 and 7 March 1991 in Saudi Arabia, Oman, The United Arab Emirates, Qatar, Jordan, Bahrain, Republic of Yemen Kuwait, Iraq, The Gulf, The Gulf of Oman, The Gulf of Aqaba, The Gulf of Suez and the Suez Canal, The Arabian Sea, The Gulf of Aden and Red Sea bounded to the east by a line from Ras Asir to a point to Ras Mauri; Cyprus and adjacent waters; The Sovereign Base Areas, the airspace and the high seas of the Eastern Mediterranean, or:

(2) Service of seven days continuously between 16 January 1991 and 28 February 1991 in Saudi Arabia, Bahrain, Kuwait, Iraq, The United Arab Emirates, Oman, Qatar, The Gulf of Oman, the north west Arabian Sea, The Gulf of Aden, The Gulf and the Red Sea, or:

(3) Service in the Kuwait Liaison Team in Kuwait on 2 August 1990.

The reverse face of this round cupro-nickel medal bears the diademed head of Elizabeth II, looking right, with an inscription reading "ELIZABETH II DEI GRATIA REGINA FID.DEF." around the inner circumference. The reverse depicts a trophy of arms surmounted by an eagle with wings spread wide, over which appear the words "THE GULF MEDAL," and beneath which, the dates "1990-91." The 1.25" wide ribbon has a ¹/₂" wide central buff stripe, which is bordered by ¹/₈" wide stripes of light blue, red, and dark blue on both sides. The suspension consists of a simple, straight suspender and ornate claw mount sweated to the medal.

Two clasps are authorized for this medal. The first reads "16 JAN TO 28 FEB 1991" for all of those entitled to the medal under clause (1) and clause (2); for those covered under clause (3), the bar reads "2 AUG 1990." When the medal is not worn, those covered under the first two clauses are authorized to wear a distinguishing rosette on the ribbon. ✕

The Gulf War Medal *(Obverse)*

The Gulf War Medal *(Reverse)*

Campaign Medal Groups

A group of two medals, including a picture of the Sergeant and his wife. To the left is the SECOND CHINA WAR MEDAL, with clasps "PEKIN 1860" and "TAKU FORTS 1860." The second medal is the ARMY LONG SERVICE/GOOD CONDUCT MEDAL.

A group of three medals awarded to the same man. From the left: THE AFGHANISTAN MEDAL with clasps "KANDAHAR," "KABUL," and "CHARASIA;" the KABUL TO KANDAHAR STAR; and the ARMY LONG SERVICE/GOOD CONDUCT MEDAL.

SERGEANT H. MURDOCH
Umtali Volunteers and
Royal Scots Fusileers

Top Left Grouping— **The QUEEN'S SOUTH AFRICA MEDAL with bars "CAPE COLONY," "ORANGE FREE STATE," "TRANSVAAL," AND "SOUTH AFRICA 1901" at left. At right is the MILITIA LONG SERVICE MEDAL.**

Top Right Grouping—**The QUEEN'S SOUTH AFRICA MEDAL with bars "CAPE COLONY," "ORANGE FREE STATE," "BELFAST," and "SOUTH AFRICA 1901." On the right is the "DELHI DERBAR MEDAL" of 1911.**

Bottom Left Grouping— **An interesting pair of medals to Sergeant H. Murdoch of the Umtali Volunteers and the Royal Scots Fusiliers. At left, the BRITISH SOUTH AFRICA COMPANY MEDAL and, at right, the QUEEN'S SOUTH AFRICA MEDAL with bars "NATAL," "ORANGE FREE STATE," "TRANSVAAL," and "SOUTH AFRICA 1901."**

A group of five medals, representing the Boer War and the First World War. From the left, the QUEEN'S SOUTH AFRICA MEDAL with bars "CAPE COLONY" and "TRANSVAAL;" the KING'S SOUTH AFRICA MEDAL with bars "SOUTH AFRICA 1901" and "SOUTH AFRICA 1902;" the BRITISH WAR MEDAL; the VICTORY MEDAL, and the ARMY LONG SERVICE/GOOD CONDUCT MEDAL.

A lovely group of six medals from the Boer war and the First World War. From the left, the QUEEN'S SOUTH AFRICA MEDAL with bars "CAPE COLONY," "ORANGE FREE STATE," and "TRANSVAAL;" the KING'S SOUTH AFRICA MEDAL with bars "SOUTH AFRICA 1901" and "SOUTH AFRICA 1902;" the 1914-15 STAR; the BRITISH WAR MEDAL; the VICTORY MEDAL; and the MEDAL FOR MERITORIOUS SERVICE.

A group of five medals to one individual: the QUEEN'S SOUTH AFRICA MEDAL with three bars, "CAPE COLONY," "ORNAGE FREE STATE," and "TRANSVAAL;" the KING'S SOUTH AFRICA MEDAL with bars "SOUTH AFRICA 1901" and "SOUTH AFRICA 1902;" the BRITISH WAR MEDAL; the VICTORY MEDAL and the ARMY LONG SERVICE/GOOD CONDUCT MEDAL.

A group of four medals showing The World War One trio and THE DELHI DERBAR MEDAL.

An outstanding trio of World War One medals, including the 1914 STAR with the "MONS BAR" on the ribbon; the BRITISH WAR MEDAL, and the VICTORY MEDAL.

A nice, clean group of five medals awarded to Private H. Duffy of the King's Own Scottish Borderers. From the First World War, the famous "trio." From the Second World War, the DEFENCE MEDAL and the National Fire Brigade Association Medal for twenty years service.

An historically significant
World War One trio, with the
1914-15 STAR named to Pte.
C. E. Willows, who enlisted in
the Canadian Princess Pat's
Canadian Light Infantry from
McGill University—the 50th
student to do so. The WAR
MEDAL and the VICTORY
MEDAL are named to Lt. C. E.
Willows, R.A.F.

Reverse of the above trio
showing the naming on the
1914-15 STAR.

A group of medals awarded to Corporal John Cassidy, 1st Battalion, Cameron Highlanders. From left, THE QUEEN'S SUDAN MEDAL; the QUEEN'S SOUTH AFRICA MEDAL with bars "CAPE COLONY," "JOHANNESBURG," "DIAMOND HILL," and "WITTEBERGEN;" the KING'S SOUTH AFRICA MEDAL with bars "SOUTH AFRICA 1901" and "SOUTH AFRICA 1902;" THE 1914-15 STAR; THE WAR MEDAL; the VICTORY MEDAL and the KHEDIVE'S SUDAN MEDAL with bars "THE ATBARA" and "KHARTOUM." The group is surmounted with the badge of the Cameron Highlanders.

And so we end for now, but know that this is not the final chapter. For there will be more battles fought, more tyrants conquered, and more medals won. There will be collectors then as now, and what they see as newly won on the field of honor will be part of yet another moment in history, to be stored and cherished in honor of the valor of each recipient and the cause for which they fought.

RWDB
1996

Value Guide

Values vary immensely according to a number of factors, including: condition of the piece; whether or not the medal is named; to whom it is named; the unit with which the individual served; the number of bars (if any); and the battles for which the bars were awarded.

The location of the market will also impact a particular medal's value, as will the economic conditions prevailing. All of these variables make it virtually impossible to create an accurate value list, but we can offer a **guide.**

The values listed below reflect a range of what one could realistically expect to pay at retail or at an auction. A medal could be at either the upper or lower end of the value bracket within which it falls. Bear in mind that this listing is, however, **only a guide**, and the author accepts no responsibility for any gain or loss the reader may experience as a result of using this guide.

Medals are identified by name, with the range of value in U.S. dollars ($) and British pounds (£) identified by a letter of the alphabet, as follows:

A - up to $60 . . . . (£ 40)

B - $60 to $100 . . . . (£ 40 to 70)

C - $100 to $250 . . . . (£ 70 to 170)

D - $250 to $500 . . . . . . (£ 170 to 340)

E - $500 to $1000 . . . . . . (£ 340 to 670)

F - $1000 to $1500 . . . . . . (£ 670 to 1000)

G - In excess of $1500 . . . (£ 1000+)

Medal/Dates:	Value range:	Photo page:
Military General Service Medal (1793-1814)	F	1
Army of India Medal (1799-1826)	E	4, 5
Waterloo Medal (June 1815)	E	6
South Africa Campaign Medal (1834-53)	D	8
Ghuznee Medal (July 1839)	E	10
First China War Medal (1840-42)	D	11
Jellalabad Medal (1841-42)	E	12
Defence of Kelat-I-Ghilzie Medal (1842)	F	13
Candahar, Cabul & Ghuznee Medals (1842-43)	E	15
Scinde Campaign Medal (1843)	E	16
Gwalior Campaign Stars (1843)	D	17
Sutlej Campaign Medal (1845-46)	D	19
Punjab Campaign Medal (1848-49)	D	22
Indian General Service Medal (1854-95)	C	24
Baltic Medal (1854-55)	B	26

Medal/Dates:	Value range:	Photo page:
Crimea Medal (1854-56)	C	27
Turkish Crimea Medal (1854-56)	B	30
Indian Mutiny Medal (1857-59)	C	31
Second China War Medal (1857-60)	C	33
New Zealand Medal (1845-47, 1860-66)	D	35
Canadian General Service Medal (1866-70)	C	37
Abyssinian War Medal (1867-68)	D	38
Ashantee War Medal (1873-74)	D	40
South African War Medal (1877-79)	C	42
Afghanistan War Medal (1878-80)	C	45
Kabul to Khandahar Star (1880)	C	49
Cape of Good Hope Gen. Service Medal (1880-97)	D	50
The Egypt Medal (1882-89)	C	52, 54
The Khedive's Star (1882-91)	B	56
North West Canada Medal (1885)	D	57
East and West Africa Medal (1887-1900)	C	58
British South Africa Company's Medal (1890-97)	D	60
Central Africa Medal (1891-98)	D	62
India General Service Medal (1895-1902)	C	63, 65
Ashanti Star (1896)	C	66
Queen's Sudan Medal (1896-97)	C	67
Khedive's Sudan Medal (1896-1908)	C	68
East and Central Africa Medal (1897-99)	D	70
British North Borneo Company's Medal (1897-1937)	B	71, 72
Queen's South Africa Medal, Silver (1899-1902)	A	74
Queen's South Africa Medal, Bronze (1899-1902)	C	74
Queen's South Africa Medal, bar "Elandslaagte"	B	78
Queen's South Africa Medal, bar "Defence Of Kimberley"	B	78
Queen's South Africa Medal, bar "Defence of Mafeking"	D	79
Queen's South Africa Medal, bar "Modder River"	B	79
Queen's South Africa Medal, bar "Defence of Ladysmith"	C	79
Queen's South Africa Medal, bars "Def. of Makeking" & "Rhodesia"	E	79
Queen's South Africa Medal, bars "South Africa" & "Cape Colony"	A	80
Queen's South Africa Medal, bars "Transvaal" & "Natal"	B	80
Queen's South Africa Medal, three bars (4 examples depicted)	B	80, 81
Queen's South Africa Medal, four bars (6 examples depicted)	C	81, 82
Queen's South Africa Medal, five bars (6 examples depicted)	C	82, 83, 84
Queen's South Africa Medal, six bars (3 examples depicted)	C	84
Queen's South Africa Medal, seven bars (1 example depicted)	C	84
King's South Africa Medal (1899-1902)	A	85
Queen's Mediterranean Medal (1899-1902)	C	86

Medal/Dates:	Value range:	Photo page:
Defence of Kimberley Star (1899-1900)	B	87
Transport Medal (1899-1902)	D	88
Ashanti Medal (1900)	D	89
Third China War Medal (1900)	C	90
Africa General Service Medal (1902-56)	C	92
Africa General Service Medal, bar "Kenya"	B	93
Tibet Medal (1903-04)	B	94
Natal Medal (1906)	C	95
India General Service Medal (1908-35)	B	96
Khedive's Sudan Medal (1910)	C	99
1914 Star (1914)	A	102
1914-15 Star (1914-15)	A	103
British War Medal (1914-20)	A	105
Victory Medal (1914-18)	A	106
Territorial Force War Medal (1914-19)	A	107
General Service Medal (1918-64)	A	108 - 114
India General Service Medal (1936-39)	B	115
1939-1945 Star (1939-45)	A	116
The Atlantic Star (1939-45)	A	117
The Africa Star (1940-43)	A	118
The Pacific Star (1941-45)	A	120
The Burma Star (1941-45)	A	121
The Italy Star (1943-45)	A	122
The France and Germany Star (1944-45)	A	123
The Defence Medal (1939-45)	A	124
The War Medal (1939-45)	A	125
India Service Medal (1939-45)	A	126
Canadian Volunteer Service Medal (1939-45)	A	127
Africa Service Medal (1939-45)	A	128
Australia Service Medal (1939-45)	A	129
New Zealand Service Medal (1939-45)	A	130
South Africa Medal for War Service (1939-46)	A	131
Southern Rhodesian War Service Medal (1939-45)	B	132
The Korea Medal (1950-53)	B	133
The Korea Medal (Canada)	C	133
The United Nations Service Medal (1950-53)	A	136
Vietnam Service Medal (1964)	C	137
South Vietnam Campaign Medal (1964)	A	138
The South Atlantic Medal (1982)	B to D	139
The Gulf War Medal (1991)	D	141
Miscellaneous Groups of Medals	C to D	142 - 148

Bibliography

Barthorp, Michael. *The Anglo-Boer Wars; The British and the Afrikaners 1815-1902.* Dorset, England: Blandford Press, 1987.

Barthorp, Michael. *War on the Nile; Britain, Egypt and the Sudan 1882-1898.* Dorset, England: Blandford Press, 1984.

Barthorp, Michael. *The North-West Frontier; A Pictorial History 1839-1947.* Dorset, England: Blandford Press, 1982.

Barthorp, Michael. *The Zulu War, A Pictorial History.* Dorset, England: Blandford Press, 1980.

Bullock, David L. *Allenby's War, The Palestine-Arabian Campaigns 1916-1918.* Dorset, England: Blandford Press, 1988.

Calthorpe, Lt. Col. Somerset J. *Cadogan's Crimea.* New York: Atheneum Publishers, 1980.

Collins, Daniel F. *The Medals Yearbook A-Z, 7th Edition.* Bournemouth, England: Cobra Publishing Co., Ltd., 1986

Dorling, H. Taprell. *Ribbons and Medals, New Enlarged Edition.* New York: Doubleday & Co., Inc., 1974.

Farwell, Byron. *Queen Victoria's Little Wars.* New York: Harper & Row, 1972.

Geraghty, Tony. *This Is The S.A.S.* New York: Arco Publishers, Inc., 1983.

Gordon, Major L. L. *British Battles and Medals, 5th Edition.* London, England: Spink and Son, Ltd., 1979.

Gould, Robert W. *Campaign Medals of the British Army 1815-1972.* London, England: Arms and Armour Press, 1982.

Haythornthwaite, Philip J. *Victorian Colonial Wars.* London, England: Arms and Armour Press, 1988.

Payne, A. A. *A Handbook of British and Foreign War Medals and Decorations Awarded to the Army and Navy.* Suffolk, England: J. B. Hayward and Sons, 1981.

Thompson, Julian. *No Picnic.* New York: Hippocrene Books, 1985.